THE FIRST FIFTY YEARS OF
Christ Church Episcopal School
A JOURNEY TO REMEMBER

The Donning Company Publishers
184 Business Park Drive, Suite 206
Virginia Beach, VA 23462

Steve Mull, General Manager
Barbara Buchanan, Office Manager
Anne Cordray, Editor
Tonya Hannink, Graphic Designer
Derek Eley, Imaging Artist
Lori Kennedy, Project Research Coordinator
Tonya Hannink, Marketing Specialist
Pamela Engelhard, Marketing Advisor

Bernie Walton, Project Director

Library of Congress Cataloging-in-Publication Data

Betette Warren, Allison.
  The first fifty years of Christ Church Episcopal School : a journey to
remember / Allison Betette Warren ; illustrated by Lyndi Simms.
     p. cm.
  ISBN 978-1-57864-580-0
  1. Christ Church Episcopal School (Greenville, S.C.)--History. I. Title.
  LD7501.G78B48 2009
  373.757'27--dc22
                                      2009027190

Printed in the United States of America at Walsworth Publishing Company

Table of Contents

Foreword

I was in the eleventh grade in 1959 when Christ Church Episcopal School was born, already a matured vision in my father's mind. Arthur McCall wanted a superior education for his children and felt (probably not coincidentally, given my track record at the time) that the public schools were not providing what was needed. Fifty years later, his vision has shaped the lives of generations of leaders in communities around the world.

I feel greatly honored to have been asked to contribute to the opening pages of this 50th anniversary history of CCES. Because of college, military service, and graduate school, I missed the first twelve years of the School, but since returning to Greenville in 1971, I have been continually involved. I have personally known all five Rectors and most Heads of School. I have participated as a member of the Vestry, as Chair of the Annual Fund in its early years, as Past President of the Board of Visitors, and most recently as Vice Chairman of the School Board. This School, one of my father's greatest legacies to Greenville, has become an enduring passion in my life too.

There have been countless contributors to the School's growth, from the early leaders, Rectors, Vestry and School Board members, to those who continue to shape it today. This history covers their involvement with exceptional clarity—and brevity, since no publication of this scope could ever hope to adequately acknowledge everyone. I think that the real dynamic of CCES lies deep within the heart and soul of the students, past, present, and future, along with the parents and grandparents who encourage and enable them to learn and achieve.

Many of the 2,300-plus graduates and 3,000-plus attendees have gone on to some astonishing careers and accomplishments. The outstanding preparation for college, test scores, and athletics and arts achievements are phenomenal. These things do not just happen because there are a few shining stars, as there are in any group. It happens because an entire team of faculty, administration, coaches, students, and their families is making it happen.

Having spent 27 years in the military, I often think about leadership and what it means. I believe I observe outstanding leadership every time I visit the CCES campus. My father would be proud of the School he helped to establish so many years ago, and prouder still of the legacy of leadership training it has provided for the community where he lived and worked.

—Arthur C. McCall, Jr.
April 8, 2009

Acknowledgments

Writing this book has been a gift. It has allowed me to understand fully how many people have genuinely cared for this School. So many of them have been quiet, faithful givers who wanted nothing more than to see CCES succeed as a place to receive a strong academic and Christian foundation.

However, I could not have finished this task without the support of my family, especially my husband Jim, who was a constant cheerleader throughout the process, or my children, Jim, Sarah, and Russell, who understood when things unraveled at home. Nor could I have done it without the support of my parents, Jay and Phil Betette, whose interest in my life inspires me.

I am grateful to Golden Cavaliers Jean Cochran, Florence Pressly, Pat McCloskey, and the late Cathy Jones who first launched this project to preserve the past. I also want to thank my editor, Alice Baird, who patiently walked me through the process, helped shape the final draft, and spent hours looking for photos and writing captions. She and I both owe much to Connie Lanzl whose vision for the book was unwavering and whose direction kept us on track. I am also indebted to Barbara Carter, who read every chapter at least three times and happily; Anne Howson, whose friendship (and office space) were unexpected, cherished gifts; Jackie Suber, whose memory and research were invaluable; Kathy Corwin, for her open door, especially during the research phase; Marion Crawford for morning pep talks; and Nancy Baker, who believed in me from the start. In addition, I appreciate research assistance from Cynthia Willis and Megan Lauritzen '06, and Brandy Lindsey for her layout designs.

Finally, I thank God for giving me this opportunity and the ability to see it to completion.

The Journey Begins

Excitement swells the air on this 9th day in September 1959. Children in bobby socks and pigtails eagerly climb the concrete steps to the schoolhouses at 503, 505, and 509 East Washington Street. Embarking on a new adventure, they are the first students to attend Christ Church Episcopal School.

CHAPTER

1

On opening day, a staff of seventeen awaits 218 students, two short of the maximum number the School will accommodate this first year. Each child has taken an entrance test and scored an average grade or above, as determined necessary by **The Reverend Thomas A. Roberts**, Rector of Christ Church. There is one four-year-old kindergarten class, three five-year-old kindergarten classes, and two first-grade classes. Second, third, fourth, fifth, and sixth forms have one class each. Over half of those in attendance are Episcopalians.

The Reverend Dr. Claude Guthrie, who has only recently moved to Greenville from Wadesboro, North Carolina, is Headmaster. Recalling an old English practice, he has divided the children into forms rather than grades. The second, third, and fourth-form students are in one house. First, fifth, and sixth forms are in another, and kindergarten shares the middle building with the administrative offices.

Despite desks in place, books on shelves, and blackboards on walls, the houses still echo a domestic purpose to the children within. There are footed, cast-iron tubs in the bathrooms, coal furnaces, and mantels above blackened fireplaces. The surroundings draw such comments as, "It's kind of neat going to school in someone's living room."

At 8:20 the school day begins. Students have until 8:30 before they will be tardy. There are no electronic bells to signal a change in subjects, so teachers watch their own clocks to end each period themselves. Generally, the school day includes five fifty-minute periods as well as time for recess, lunch, assemblies, and homeroom activities.

Roberts and Guthrie have hired an exceptional teaching staff. They have set minimum requirements of a "Bachelor of Arts degree with at least 18 months work toward a Master's Degree" (Vestry minutes, June 22, 1959). To attract the strongest possible group of teachers, they have offered salaries slightly higher than those in the county schools.

In his six years as the School's first Headmaster, Father Guthrie set in place many CCES traditions that endure today, including the crest, the School motto, and the Greek-themed publication names.

Roberts insists that this added cost in salaries is necessary to the success of the new School. Whether by accident or by design, the School has in Roberts a brilliant mind for management. He is a former IBM vice president and general manager who only later decided to enter seminary. His business acumen allows him to determine a tuition that will cover an ambitious budget. The St. James Episcopal School, from which CCES has attracted many students, has been charging $15 per month. But at the outset, Roberts sets the tuition at $27.50 per month, along with a $10 testing fee and a $10 fee for textbooks.

During one summer meeting, a prospective parent in the audience calls, "You'll never get people in Greenville to pay $25 a month for their children to go to school!" But before much time passes and through collective efforts, the School of more than 200 students begins to thrive. A feeling that something significant is being born begins to drive the administration, the faculty, the students, and the parents.

By November, the students help create the first news and literary magazine, calling it *The Athenian*. It provides a place for poems, essays, and short stories from young writers in second through sixth form. An entry by seven-year-old **Jane McCall '67**, daughter of founder **Arthur C. McCall,** reads as follow:

Halloween
   Halloween is here.
   Witches are out.
   Black cats are out too.
   The boys and girls pick pumpkins.
   The boys and girls have parties.

Anne Pryor '65 in the fourth form reports on events since the start of school. She describes a visit from Duke Power Company and how her class is studying Benjamin Franklin in groups. She concludes her article by eagerly telling all about the upcoming Halloween party.

Guthrie also writes a column announcing his plans for the year, among them the publication of a yearbook that will carry the Greek name, *The Hellenian*. He adds that it will require everyone to have a "school-day" picture taken soon.

CHAPEL

Most mornings, first through sixth-form students leave the schoolhouses to walk to the chapel on Church Street. Three times a week they participate in liturgical worship services according to *The Book of Common Prayer* of the Episcopal Church. The four-year and five-year kindergarten classes engage in formal services twice a week. As is customary, women and girls cover their heads with white chapel caps the School provides. It is also common for teachers and students to genuflect before the altar upon entering a pew.

This near-daily gathering becomes central to the identity of CCES from the outset. Former seminary classmates at the University of the South in Sewanee, Tennessee, Roberts and Guthrie both believe that it is the combined responsibility of the Church and the School to provide an atmosphere in which "proper experiences may be part of daily living. This implies that in all relationships in the School life, the essence of our Christian faith should be evident." (Guthrie's *Lecture I* to faculty)

The children return from chapel in single-file lines. Some walk on the sidewalk and others take the caretaker road through the graveyard, talking and laughing as they go. On one particular day **Page Scovil Hoyle** (1959–73) stops to remark on the Confederate soldiers buried in the cemetery. A boy who has recently moved to Greenville from the North blurts out, "Nah, nah, the Yankees won the war!" Complete pandemonium ensues, and the children begin a wild chase through the graveyard.

Back inside, there is a flurry of shedding coats and caps before conversations subside. Then each class settles into an academic routine beginning with the Pledge of Allegiance. First through sixth-form students follow a continuing curriculum of reading, writing, science, math, and language arts. No class has more than twenty children, "in order that each student receive the necessary amount of time from the teacher to do his best work," according to Roberts.

RECESS

Weather permitting, the children have recess in the double yard behind numbers 503 and 505 East Washington Street. There is adequate room for play, but the ground is rocky and hard, and black cinders from old kitchen stoves show up on skinned knees and elbows. The students themselves are oblivious to their rough playground. Rather they anticipate recess as if no place were finer. In the same spirit, teachers join in games of kickball, jump-rope, and "no-hands," as they call soccer.

A Tribute to
JEAN COCHRAN (1959–95)

*I remember well the hustle and excitement of opening day as our family enrolled one child in third grade [**H. Neel Hipp, Jr. '66**] and another in first [**Mary Ladson Hipp '68**], both of whom had worked up from St. James. **Jean Cochran** was teaching first grade as she had done at St. James, and as our family enrollees grew to five, each one passed through her capable hands. As a result, we have a family of eager readers that stretches into the third generation.*

—Jane Hipp

Known as CCES's "first teacher," Jean Cochran worked in the School's classrooms from day one teaching first grade for thirty years. For the next five years of her tenure she served as Admissions Director as well as Assistant Director of the Lower School. In 1995, in recognition of her extraordinary service to the School, the "Cochran Room" in the Middle School was dedicated in her honor and she was named *Teacher-Administrator Emerita*, the only faculty member in the School ever to be so honored.

In the spring of 1959 Father Roberts approached Cochran, who at the time was Director of the Episcopal Day School at St. James, to help start a parish school at Christ Church. Such was her commitment to raising the level of education in the community that she immediately agreed, even though she had two small children (and a third one later) of her own to consider. She spent the summer months preparing three vacant clapboard houses for the arrival of students in September.

To Jean, CCES was an extended family. It was a place to foster relationships that would have an impact for a lifetime. She understood the significance of shaping young minds and took this role seriously.

Mornings in Jean's room began with prayer and a devotional reading. Then there was formal instruction in all of the basic subject areas, with an ever-so-slight preference for phonics. Jean believed earnestly in the importance of phonics in learning to read.

Jean insisted that her young students were mannerly. Repeatedly, she would remind them to tuck in shirttails, remove hats indoors, wipe muddy feet, wash sticky hands, and, if necessary, flush the commode. But Jean had a sense of humor too.

"Life in Mrs. Cochran's class was always exciting," said **Dr. Keith Strausbaugh '83**, remembering a particular day when Cochran mixed up the contents of all her students' lunches. She had even filled some of them with nonsensical items, such as tennis balls wrapped in foil. "At the peak of chaos, Mrs. Cochran and someone from McDonald's arrived with a huge box of what would now be called Happy Meals. I can still remember the excitement and joy of that moment," Strausbaugh said.

CCES's "First Teacher," Jean Cochran, was known for her insistence on order and good manners—and for her soft heart.

"I loved every day at CCES!" Cochran once told a group enthusiastically. And she did. Her love was infectious too. The faculty fed off it, the students felt it, and the parents saw evidence of it in their children. She was one of those teachers who knew from the outset that she belonged here. No place on earth was more special or important to her.

A page from the 1960 *Hellenian*, published during the School's first year, showing the three houses where CCES began, and the Christ Church Parish House before it was expanded to accommodate the School.

ENRICHMENT

Sixth-form teacher **Rufus Bethea** has been hired at the recommendation of Christ Church members **Sumner Williams** and Arthur McCall, who want a man to teach the older students and to serve as assistant athletic director. Bethea has six years of summer camp experience in addition to military training that make him ideal for the position. Upon his arrival, he begins to take fifth and sixth-form boys to the YMCA for field sports. A gymnasium is part of the new Parish House plan and will provide a place for a sports program. But for now, the lack of space and equipment is simply an obstacle to overcome.

All CCES children learn music from **Ruth Watson** (1959–66), who studied at Juilliard School of Music. Once a week, they walk to the Parish House for instruction in a small room hardly bigger than a coat closet. Watson teaches her students how to chant the "Plain Songs" from *The Book of Common Prayer* and to sing Episcopal hymns. She also writes operettas in order to include every child in a spring performance.

In addition, first through sixth-form students spend two thirty-minute periods each week learning French from Watson. She walks room-to-room teaching them basic phrases and songs, laying a foundation for future foreign language study.

Parishioner **Genevieve Shirley**, Director of Christian Education at Christ Church, voluntarily teaches Christian education. She persuades Page Scovil to teach Christian education to the four-year kindergarten class and all three five-year kindergarten classes without pay. It would be two years before Scovil was placed on the School's payroll.

Shirley's husband, **Tom**, gives weekly folk-dancing lessons at no charge. He also oversees the custodial responsibilities. This couple is among the many parishioners who simply want to contribute their time and talents to a school now bursting with promise.

DISMISSAL

At 2:30, school dismisses. Guthrie reminds all teachers that "no class is kept overtime, especially at the end of the day when students are to take busses." Dismissal time is welcomed by the teachers, who have not had a break all day. They will stay a while longer, though, for there is much planning to do to achieve "academic excellence." Already there is camaraderie among the faculty, so no one is in a hurry to leave.

The community that is Christ Church Episcopal School is beginning to take shape.

ARTHUR McCALL

THOMAS ROBERTS

CLAUDE GUTHRIE

Architects of the Journey

They began with the vision of a Christ-centered and academically rigorous education. It would be a new mission of Christ Church. Without maps to guide them, they charted their course with daring and resolve. The direction they set in the early days continues to fortify the School's identity.

CHAPTER

2

The cross and anchor of faith guided the founders of the School.

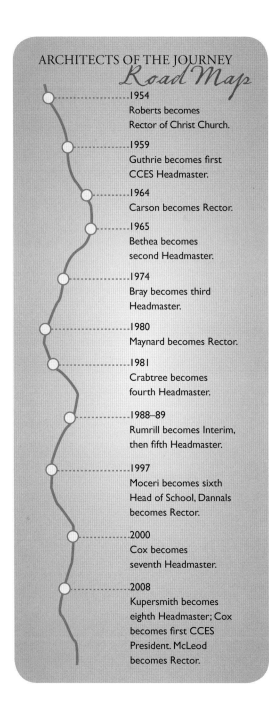

ARCHITECTS OF THE JOURNEY
Road Map

1954
Roberts becomes
Rector of Christ Church.

1959
Guthrie becomes first
CCES Headmaster.

1964
Carson becomes Rector.

1965
Bethea becomes
second Headmaster.

1974
Bray becomes third
Headmaster.

1980
Maynard becomes Rector.

1981
Crabtree becomes
fourth Headmaster.

1988–89
Rumrill becomes Interim,
then fifth Headmaster.

1997
Moceri becomes sixth
Head of School, Dannals
becomes Rector.

2000
Cox becomes
seventh Headmaster.

2008
Kupersmith becomes
eighth Headmaster; Cox
becomes first CCES
President. McLeod
becomes Rector.

It is often said that each individual who headed CCES blessed the School with just the right talents at just the right time. Each possessed the gifts or personality fitting to the challenges of his or her administration. These seven individuals, **Claude Guthrie**, **Rufus Bethea**, **Allen Bray**, **Ben Crabtree**, **Jim Rumrill**, **Ellen Moceri**, and **Lee Cox**, came to us almost providentially and dedicated themselves fully to the mission before them.

Similarly, five Christ Church Rectors have provided guidance at different stages in the School's development. Until the official separation of Church and School in April 2001, these men shouldered the responsibility of leading one of the largest Episcopal churches in the country, while also overseeing the affairs of a growing parish school. Rectors **Tom Roberts**, **Tom Carson**, **Dennis Maynard**, and **Bob Dannals** all played important roles in making the School what it is today. As a member of the School Board, the current Rector, **The Rev. Harrison McLeod**, continues to have a voice in the School's affairs.

And while these leaders made lasting contributions of their own, they also knew to surround themselves with highly capable people. They understood the first maxim of good leadership—that "no man is an island"—and they relied upon the strength of those on the Vestry, School Board, administration, faculty, and parents.

IN THE BEGINNING

In the beginning, Arthur Crosswell McCall had a vision to form an independent school in Greenville, South Carolina, that would provide unparalleled academic excellence. His own children were attending the Donaldson School on Tindal Avenue, where some classes had as many as forty-five students. He gathered support for his idea quickly and called a meeting of interested parents in his office at South Carolina National Bank on a brisk January evening in 1959. Among those who attended were **Emory Brown**, **Mary Simms Furman**, **Calhoun Jean Hipp**, **Jane Hipp**, **Wilkins** and **Jackie Norwood**, **Arthur** and **Kathryn McCall**, and **James** and **Florence Pressly** (1968–74). Together, this group pledged $77,000 toward creating an independent school, a sum that would exceed $650,000 today.

Two months later, the Christ Church Vestry nominated McCall to sit on the board of the Episcopal Day School. Since 1956, the small school had been a community mission of four local Episcopal churches, including St. James, Church of the Redeemer, St. Andrews, and Christ Church. The Vestry believed that McCall's interest in private education would be an asset.

The President of the Episcopal Day School Board, **Robert W. Toomey**, wanted to expand the school into a non-parochial Greenville Day School. To this end, he asked Christ Church for rental space in its new parish house. However, the Christ

Church Vestry was opposed to leasing the new Sunday School building for a non-parochial school and voted against the request. Their decision sealed the fate of Greenville Day School, for it had run out of options.

Later that month, the Greenville Day School Board approached The Reverend Thomas (Tom) A. Roberts (Rector, 1956–64) about assuming the responsibilities of the young school "with no strings attached." Roberts was receptive.

On June 22, 1959, he prayerfully opened a meeting in the Church's Arrington Room to promote the idea to the Vestry. Those present were **The Reverend Robert N. Lockard**; **C. E. Hatch, Jr.**; **I. L. Donkle**; **W. D. Asnip**; **J. H. Bringhurst, Jr.**; **Al F. Burgess**; **O. Perry Earle, Jr.**; **Frank H. Gibbs, Jr.**; **Harold P. Goller, Jr.**; **Gaston Jennings**; **Dr. J. W. Jervey, Jr.**; **August W. Smith**; **H. R. Turner**; and **W. Harrison Trammell, Jr.**

Roberts spoke of the ninety-five displaced pupils in kindergarten through second grade at the Episcopal Day School who could serve as a foundation for a new school. He said that if "proper housing could be found, it will be planned that a third grade, and possibly fourth and fifth grades would be added this year." He predicted, "with Christ Church solidly behind the program, and if grades through the sixth can be offered, the enterprise should be successful."

Roberts assessed the necessary costs. He said a "third clergyman would be needed to operate the School without the disservice of the communicants of Christ Church," and the expense of a Headmaster could be estimated as follows:

Salary and expenses of Headmaster	*$10,000 per year*
Overhead, including services	*$ 7,500*
	$17,500

"In addition, nine teachers may be required at a total of $24,975 per year. If the anticipated enrollment should materialize, it is estimated that we would still face a $1,250 deficit for the first year's operation," he said. Roberts set tuition for each grade level at $27.50 per month for first through fifth grades, $18 per month for four-year kindergarten, and $20 per month for five-year kindergarten. He also suggested a $10 testing fee and, once enrolled, a $10 book fee.

After considerable discussion, Donkle moved that the Vestry of Christ Church accept the request of the Greenville Day School Board to acquire the Episcopal Day School. Vestry members Hatch and Burgess proposed the new name "Christ Church Day School," and Vestry members Jervey and Jennings motioned that the word *Episcopal* replace the word *Day*. Christ Church Episcopal School (CCES) was born.

THE REVEREND CLAUDE E. GUTHRIE (HEADMASTER, 1959–65)

Less than a month later, the Senior Warden reported that The Reverend Claude E. Guthrie from Wadesboro, North Carolina, had accepted the position of Headmaster. With a bachelor's degree in music from North Texas State College, a bachelor's degree in divinity from Sewanee: The University of the South, two years toward a PhD from the University of North Carolina, and thirteen years of teaching experience, he possessed the academic and spiritual qualifications to lead a parish school.

From the day he arrived in mid-July, Guthrie was intent on establishing a strong foundation. He knew his direction would likely have a lasting impact on the course of the School. In August, the Vestry voted to give Guthrie full voice in future meetings.

On Tuesday, August 25, 1959, an article appeared in *The Greenville News*, officially announcing the School and its purposes. "The principles in the day school will be the same as in the Sunday school," Guthrie said. "All the Christian education taught in this school will be as the Episcopal Church holds it.…Our aim is to have a school where each individual student will be able to move at his maximum rate. The aim of our academic level will be that consistently attained in private schools."

Five days after CCES opened, the Vestry heard an encouraging report: "The children and parents are apparently satisfied. Over fifty percent of the children are Episcopalians. All classes are filled, with the exception of one child in the sixth grade. All children passed admission tests, scoring average or above."

Not one to waste time, Guthrie turned his attention to details that would help distinguish the new School. Declaring the "School will follow a Greek motif," he

In his letter of resignation, Guthrie wrote, "My first goal was to establish a school of first-rate quality. We accomplished that in the six years I was there."

adopted a motto borrowing from the Greek phrase, "The Beautiful is Difficult," or "High quality involves hard work," which he incorporated into a crest. He started a literary magazine, calling it *The Athenian*, and he printed the first *Hellenian* yearbook all by the close of the first year.

The second year built upon the first. In September 1960 CCES moved from its temporary headquarters in three houses on Washington Street to the new Church Parish House, where a seventh and eighth grade were added. The new accommodations included sophisticated classrooms, a library, a gymnasium, a dining room, and playground equipment. Enrollment climbed to 400 students.

With the gymnasium, an athletics program was now possible. Guthrie, together with sixth-form teacher Rufus Bethea, established an athletic policy "encouraging all students to participate and not just the talented few."

Ninth form was added in 1961 to allow for a complete junior high school. (At the time, local public schools grouped grades 7-9 in "junior high schools.") In a memo to the Vestry Committee, Guthrie recommended the addition, "so as to provide for transfer of students to local public high schools directly rather than to one year in junior high."

On August 28, 1962, the Vestry created a subcommittee of the board "to subscribe to the purposes of the School." In addition to McCall, Roberts, and Guthrie, the members of this first group were Sidney Bruce, Jr., William (Bill) K. Stephenson, Ardis Parrot, and Harrison Trammell. This group of seven oversaw all decisions involving the young School for the next two years. Roberts set forth the purposes of the new venture: "to provide Christian education as a definite part of a child's intellectual and social development, and to provide the facilities and faculty necessary to offer a high-standard educational program." (*Letter to Patrons,* June 26, 1959)

In April 1964 Roberts resigned as Rector of Christ Church. He wrote a farewell letter to the CCES parents conveying his pride in the faculty and students. He added that CCES had been accepted into the Mid-South Association of Independent Schools, recognition of the School's excellence.

This has been one of the greatest and most gratifying challenges in my ministry here, and I leave the job as Rector of the parish and of the School with a firm assurance that that which was started in faith has grown by His grace and shall continue to do so in the future.

—Tom Roberts

In July 1964 The Reverend Thomas (Tom) H. Carson, Jr. (Rector, 1964–80) followed Roberts as Rector of Christ Church. Carson would lead the School through many trials and triumphs for nearly fifteen years.

During Father Carson's nearly fifteen years as Rector, he established the Cavalier Campus and built the Upper School.

Almost immediately, Carson faced a growing demand for a high school. In 1965, he hired a consulting firm in New York to determine if Greenville could support a parochial upper school. The firm concluded that it could not. Instead, it "proposed that the upper school be church-oriented but not church-controlled—in short, [it should] be a community school." It said, "Christ Church has uses for funds in order to meet pressing needs of the Church that have nothing to do with the School. Consequently, the Church should not be allowed to carry the load of the School alone."

The School was now the primary mission of the Church. Moreover, it was extremely successful, even though very young. Reluctant to establish a community school that was not "church-controlled," the Vestry, in response to the consultant's report, decided to wait.

In 1965, Guthrie resigned as Headmaster to become an Archdeacon for the Diocese. Father Carson accepted his decision "with much regret" for Carson knew Guthrie's leadership had been invaluable.

My first goal was to establish a school of first-rate quality. We accomplished that in the six years I was there. Another goal was the overall success of the School. That was also accomplished in the first six years. The School had an enviable reputation in the county among both public and private schools....

One goal I had for the School was not realized while I was there and that was integration. I had the distinct feeling that the School did not exist for the purposes of segregation. The people really wanted a better educational program for their children, especially those who were markedly above average in academic achievement. I never felt that the school community would have any problem with integration in that kind of educational environment.

—Claude Guthrie

RUFUS H. BETHEA
(HEADMASTER, 1965–74)

In May 1965 Carson hired Rufus H. Bethea to be the next Headmaster. Bethea had left his teaching position at CCES three years earlier to become Assistant Headmaster at the Summit School in Winston Salem, North Carolina. The agreement between the two gentlemen was established in two brief personal letters. It also marked the beginning of a friendship that would benefit the School for nearly a decade.

CCES underwent relatively few physical changes between 1965–68. During these years, it settled into its identity, maintained a near-full enrollment, and secured its reputation in the community.

Bethea became a father figure to his faculty. He regularly held cookouts at Paris Mountain State Park on Friday evenings for all staff and their families. He also sent them to annual regional and national teachers conferences to encourage professional growth and friendships. To allow his staff time to travel to these events, he thought nothing of asking the Board of Trustees for an unscheduled holiday.

"He created an atmosphere where people truly cared for one another," said Benjamin M. Crabtree, who at the time was a faculty member but would eventually become the School's fourth Headmaster in 1981. Crabtree remembered his first CCES contract as no more than a handshake and a handwritten agreement on a piece of spiral notepaper.

Bethea gave equal care to his students. He wanted to know the parents and the name of every child. To get to know them better, he promoted class trips to Williamsburg, Charleston, and Washington, D.C., by the seventh, eighth, and ninth grades respectively. To this day, the seventh-grade trip to Williamsburg continues. He also worked tirelessly to build the athletic program he had begun earlier with Guthrie.

In his nine years as Headmaster, Rufus Bethea became a father figure to the faculty, regularly holding cookouts at Paris Mountain State Park on Friday evenings for staff and their families.

Upper School Moving Days,
1971 AND 2002

In 1971, in drenching rain, a restless bunch of juniors and seniors abandoned the gypsy-like existence that had taken them to classes at the Cleveland Street YMCA for a year and then at Textile Hall for two months while waiting on the completion of the Upper School. On October 18 everyone, including parents and those in the administration, helped to move a mountain of Upper School books and materials from downtown to the Cavalier Campus almost seven miles away. With classes scheduled in the new building the following day, it was a massive effort to complete the move in twenty-four hours. But once settled, Student Council President **Eddie Buck '72** noted, "This was Paradise! We had our own building and our own athletic fields."

Thirty-one years later, in 2002, the rain held off under gray skies as students and teachers again moved Upper School items, this time only about seventy yards away, to the new Upper School building. Wearing purple tee shirts that read "The Beautiful is Difficult: To Move," a play on the School's motto, they carted hundreds of boxes from the library, 450 desks, more than one hundred computers, and the personal collections of forty-two faculty and staff members. Students and faculty transported at least 80 percent of the building's contents and were seen hoisting everything from the mounted wildlife trophies from **Reggie Titmas**'s biology lab to computers and cables. Some even made fast work of the back-and-forth between the old and new Upper Schools by gliding on skateboards.

Alex Ritter '03 pulls a handtruck piled with boxes into the elevator of the new three-story Upper School in 2002.

A student assists French teacher John Gildersleeve in loading a truck during the move to the new Upper School in 1971.

Former Vestry member and School Board Chair Randolph Stone reminisces about negotiations with the Wenwood Investment Group in 1970 for land on which to build the Upper School.

Bethea knew which students were struggling in their studies too. In a November 1966 meeting with the Board of Trustees, he told them, "A problem called dyslexia exists with 16 percent of the school population. There might be as many as 30 children in Christ Church Episcopal School handicapped by dyslexia and its effects." He asked to be allowed to find training for a faculty member who could "offer assistance to our students in the summer."

Among his many contributions to CCES, O. Perry Earle, Jr., was present at the Vestry meeting in 1959 when the Church voted to form a parochial school, and he was instrumental in finding and purchasing land for an upper school a decade later.

Unafraid to challenge the status quo, Bethea accepted the first African American students in 1967, when enrollment was 411 students, mostly Episcopalians. He wrote to parents saying, "One note about next year: the policy of Christ Church Episcopal School since its inception has been one of being open to any qualified student without regard to race, creed or ethnic origin in accordance with the canons of the Episcopal Church. We wish to advise you that our first Negro child has been enrolled in the Primer class for the school year 1968–69." **Bill Gibson**, **William Johnson,** and **Denise Peters** began the following fall, creating a more diverse student body.

Meanwhile, the idea for an upper school continued to surface without resolution in board meetings. The existing Parish House could not hold three additional grades, but demand for a high school was growing. Carson appointed a committee to study the situation, even though the roadblocks seemed endless.

Then on Christmas Eve 1968, the discouraged Rector received a telephone call from **Jean Louise Reamsbottom McKissick**. She told him she wanted to give her house at 800 Crescent Avenue as a basis for an endowment for a "church-related high school." But, she said, CCES would have to begin construction within three years of her death or the property would pass to Presbyterian College. A grateful Carson directed Perry Earle to chair a committee, including **Ben Norwood** and Harrison Trammell, to find a building site. Carson had the foresight to insist upon at least fifty acres to allow for "adequate athletic fields and future buildings," but finding such acreage in town was difficult.

News that a new upper school might become a reality moved everyone to action. Knowing the Parish House would nearly burst with the addition of more students, Bethea nonetheless agreed to Carson's request for adding a tenth grade in the fall of 1969. The thinking was that a building would be ready the following fall for grades 10, 11 and, eventually, 12.

As it happened, the Upper School was not completed until November 1971 because undeveloped property near town was hard to find. After much searching, Earle approached a group of friends who together owned a tract of undeveloped land they called the Wenwood property. It met the fifty-acre minimum and, although some thought it was too far from the Church, its location was satisfactory.

Jean Louise Reamsbottom McKissick brightened Rector Tom Carson's 1968 Christmas by bequeathing her home to the School for the purpose of building a high school.

In 1992–93 the impressive home was used as a showhouse to raise funds.

Headmaster Rufus Bethea confers with a student in his office in 1971.

Carson then appointed **John Douglas** to help Earle negotiate the sale. He also directed **E. Randolph Stone** to handle the deeds. Because the land was more expensive than expected, Douglas and Earle negotiated that for every acre they bought, the sellers would give them an acre at no charge. The Church acquired the first fifteen-acre tract in July of 1970, enabling construction to begin a few months later.

All the while, the School continued to operate as planned. However, the Parish House could not possibly hold an eleventh grade. The administration had no choice but to find a temporary venue for the Upper School during the 1970–71 school year. The YMCA on Cleveland Street, which had provided fields for athletic competition for nearly a decade, became the best option. And so it was that Bethea and Carson guided displaced tenth and eleventh graders through "Christ High at the Y," as students came to call it.

When the time came for the new academic year to begin, the Upper School building was still not complete. "A rainy August and a dearth of brick masons have put things a little behind schedule," Bethea told parents. "The site and the building for the Upper School exceed our fondest dreams. Although we will be a little late moving in, it will probably be a great adventure making the move with the students after the beginning of school," he said.

Once again, the administration scrambled to locate temporary quarters for grades 8–12, finding them at a warehouse known as Textile Hall. Conditions were modest, at best. Chapel services took place on a balcony, bathrooms were on the ground floor, air-conditioning was nonexistent, and an air horn signaled when it was time to change classes. Only a dedicated faculty and anticipation about the coming building made the situation bearable. **Georgia Frothingham**, **Cathy Jones**, **Florence Pressly**, and **Mary Roper** were among the teachers who kept order and maintained a sense of humor throughout the unusual months.

At last, moving day arrived on Monday, October 18, 1971. Amid pouring rain, with parents, teachers, and students hauling cartons and furniture, the new campus at 100 Cavalier Drive came to life. According to newly hired English teacher **Jackie Fowler (née Suber)** (1971–2004), "The new CCES Upper School, with its open classrooms, individual approach to learning, and a growing high school population, was on the cutting edge of what was happening in education in the late sixties and early seventies."

Two months later, on Sunday, November 28, 1971, the Bishop of Upper South Carolina, **The Right Reverend John A. Pinckney**, dedicated the lone brick building that was now the Upper School. Bethea and School Board Chair Ben Norwood stood as honorary gatekeepers for the "Opening the Door" ceremony. Twenty-two years after opening, CCES had at last completed its mission to offer twelve grades.

Over the next year and a half, Bethea continued to develop the academic and athletic reputation of the School. Enrollment reached nearly 800 and a spirit of unity prevailed, even with two separate campuses. Still, the board was anxious to complete the plans to provide for athletics and fine arts. In 1973 ground was broken for the construction of a new field house and for the addition of an arts and commons wing to the Upper School.

In January 1974, having successfully overseen major expansion, Bethea announced his resignation to become Headmaster of Christ School in Arden, North Carolina.

> *I leave CCES with only the greatest love for all involved and greatest confidence that it will continue to grow in stature and be a leader in the schools of this country. …I can never say too much about the tremendous support that I have received from the Rector, Vestry, School Board and the students and you, the parents. No one could ask for more.*
>
> —Rufus Bethea

Students, too, clearly revered Bethea. A dedication in *The Setting Sun* read, "Physically the man stands tall: 6'3". But height is not what we are concerned with when we speak of Mr. Rufus H. Bethea. We speak of him as a man who stands tall in every way, a giant in any endeavor."

In 2004 Bethea was named *Headmaster Emeritus* for his exceptional leadership.

A Tribute to
NANCY BAKER (1974–2004)

Nancy Baker arrived at CCES in 1974 when Rufus Bethea was Headmaster. She came to teach accounting and typing for the new Upper School business program. At the same time, she worked as Financial Secretary for the Cavalier Campus until Jim Rumrill persuaded her to be Assistant to the Headmaster in 1993. Given her reputation for organization, accuracy, and professionalism, Ellen Moceri and Lee Cox retained her in this important position. For many years, she supported those at the top with precision, grace, and tact. Baker retired in 2004 after devoting thirty years to seven administrations.

Today, Baker is a primary keeper of School history, because few others know the inner workings of CCES as well. The reception area for the President/Headmaster's offices has been named in her honor so that her dedication will never be forgotten.

Head of School Ellen Moceri proclaimed May 22, 2002, "Nancy Baker Day." On Nancy's retirement from CCES in 2003, President George W. Bush sent a congratulatory letter on White House stationery, courtesy of Tucker Eskew '79 (then Director of the White House Office of Global Communications).

THE REVEREND CANON ALLEN F. BRAY III (HEADMASTER, 1974–81)

In February 1974 **Ellison S. McKissick II**, Bill Stephenson, and Carson returned from a three-day trip to find a new Headmaster. According to McKissick, The Reverend Canon Allen F. Bray III "met all the qualifications submitted by both the faculty and the Board and that if the Board and Vestry were willing, we would issue him a call."

Soon afterward, Carson announced that Bray had accepted the post. Bray had a bachelor's degree from Trinity College in Hartford, Connecticut, and a bachelor of divinity degree from the Virginia Theological Seminary. He also possessed a master's degree in sacred theology from Seabury Western Theological Seminary in Evanston, Illinois. He had served as Headmaster at three different schools, beginning in 1960 with Culver Military at Culver, Indiana, and he had written several publications, including *The Return of Self Concern, Religion and the Private School* and *Christian Education in Church-Related and Independent Schools.*

Eager to begin, Bray submitted the first of many detailed reports to the board just weeks after his arrival. In his opinion, the academic standards were not rigorous enough. By the start of the school year, Bray increased the number of sections a teacher taught to five, created an advisee system in place of the homeroom structure, added department heads, and initiated plans to move the seventh grade to the Upper School.

Bray also reduced the budget, despite the fact that CCES now managed a larger campus with increased expenses. The years in which operational costs were confined to salaries and supplies had come to an end, necessitating a greater awareness of spending. There were also growing concerns over enrollment for the upcoming year, as national projections forecast a weakening economy.

In October 1974 Bray assigned **Charles (Pete) D. Cooper** to the position of Assistant Headmaster for the Upper School. A member of the faculty since 1971, Cooper would now

From the start, Headmaster Canon Bray worked to elevate academic standards at the School.

oversee Upper School affairs and act as Headmaster in Bray's absence. He would also continue as teacher, coach, college counselor, Coordinator of Student Activities, and Director of Admissions for the Upper School.

In December Arthur McCall reported to the Vestry that his committee was working to reduce the building debt substantially, and he hoped to reduce it still more by month's end. The Board of Trustees approved Bray's recommendation to raise the tuition $100 per student for the upcoming school year, and Carson recommended contacting parents for donations of their Enrollment Certificates, which parents were required to purchase to help fund the new buildings. (These certificates are discussed further on page 52.)

Bray announced the tuition increase with pragmatism. He told them, "This figure includes a subscription to the newspaper, the yearbook, and the literary magazine. It includes the athletic fee for Middle and Upper School students as well as free admission to all home varsity athletic contests. More importantly, it includes a tuition insurance provision that guarantees the School full tuition and a high percentage of return of the unexpended tuition to the parents in the event of illness, transfer or required withdrawal."

Then in March, Bray announced that **Montague (Monte) G. Ball, Jr.,** had accepted the position of Director of the Middle School. This new position was part of Bray's plan to insert more structure in the administration. An alumnus of Choate and the University of Virginia with a master's degree from the University of North Carolina, Ball oversaw seventh, eighth, and ninth-grade affairs with humor and an endearing style. His "verbal harpoons," his "armchair tour of the world" geography class, and James Thurber stories captivated students from the start. "He had a way with kids like no other teacher I have encountered before or since," said **Bill Dykes '82**. "Mr. Ball treated me like an adult friend."

Less than a month later, **Charles J. Miller** unexpectedly resigned as Director of the Lower School to take a Headmaster position in Camden, South Carolina. He had been Assistant Headmaster to Rufus Bethea before becoming the Lower School Director, and he had provided much stability during this period of expansion and transition.

Bray picked Miller's replacement from his staff. **Eugenia Howard** had taught at CCES since 1964 and had proved to be a capable manager as chair of a Faculty Study Committee. She, along with Ball and Cooper, would constitute an important layer of leadership beneath Bray.

In the meantime, the Parents Organization, begun in 1971, also decided to organize itself officially. CCES parents drew up a constitution declaring their purpose to assist "the Board of Trustees, the Headmaster, and the faculty in the educational program of the school, to utilize the talents and services offered by the parents of children enrolled, and to enhance the interest of parents in their children's educational environment."

With significantly more structure in place, Bray turned again to curriculum matters. He and his staff worked tirelessly, sometimes meeting until midnight, to ensure that the students at CCES had every possible academic and athletic opportunity. Under his guidance, the art and music programs grew as well.

Enrollment, however, continued to decline. Inflation, a recession, and high unemployment began to take their toll on the local economy, and everywhere people were forced to cut expenses.

In April 1978 Bray reported to the School Executive Committee that 330 students had re-enrolled. And while that number would increase to over 500 before the new school year began, the situation was troubling. Just a few years before, enrollment had been nearly double. In addition to adverse economic conditions, Bray said, "public schools in the area [were] becoming more acceptable for various reasons."

The Church came to the School's aid late in December of 1978 with a "Venture in Mission" (VIM) campaign, whose purpose was to raise $1 million by the end of March 1979, half for the Church's mission projects and half for CCES. Arthur McCall, Sr., chaired Advanced Gifts. **Arthur (Artie) McCall, Jr.,** chaired VIM at the Church, and **Macon Patton, Sr.,** took charge of the non-parishioner campaign. The Parents Organization sponsored a dinner at McCall Field House to explain the campaign to CCES parents. Another dinner for parishioners took place at Memorial Auditorium, with *Gone with the Wind* star Olivia deHaviland as keynote speaker. It was a collective push by parishioners, parents, faculty, students, and the administration to rescue the struggling School. By May 1979, the VIM campaign had received $600,000 in pledges. Local businesses had responded to this corporate campaign, indicating community support. Equally encouraging was the fact that students at CCES had substantially exceeded the national SAT average that year, and eleven of the sixty-eight students in the senior class had been recognized either as National Merit Finalists or Semifinalists.

In March 1979, after a decade and a half of consummate dedication to the Church and the School, the Vestry accepted Carson's resignation with "deep regret." He had been called to the position of Executive for Stewardship and Development for the Episcopal Church in New York. With characteristic graciousness, Carson expressed his gratitude toward Christ Church, saying that "only the call of God and the Holy Spirit would ever have made me consider any other job."

Carson had become less involved in the daily affairs of CCES since Bray's arrival. Nonetheless, he remained keenly interested and instrumental from a distance. He thoughtfully appointed members of the Vestry to the School Board who would honor the founding principles of the School, and he continued to take part in hiring every member of the faculty and staff.

The Vestry appointed **The Reverend E. Cannon McCreary** to temporarily assume many of the Rector's responsibilities. Then it formed a search committee for Carson's replacement.

In 1980 **Edmund L. Potter**, **H. R. Stephenson, Jr.**, **Louise Oxner**, and **Elizabeth (Lizzy) Sterling** returned from Texas after meeting The Reverend Dr. Dennis R. Maynard (Rector, 1980–95) and his wife, Nancy. Favorably impressed with Maynard's success at his present parish, the group made a motion to offer him the Rector's position.

The Maynards arrived in town to find great optimism in spite of economic challenges and leadership changes. It helped that alumni were beginning to return to Greenville as CCES supporters. In 1980 **Marguerite Ramage Wyche '65** submitted a proposal to form an alumni association.

The following year, Maynard concluded that "the Parish and School should each carry its own weight financially." He felt he could not hire necessary clergy for the Church because of the financial commitment to the School. Maynard believed the declining enrollment was no longer a matter just for the Vestry and School Board to solve. Rather it was a problem for the whole school community. Bray opposed his thinking on the grounds that since the School was a "true parochial school and the primary mission of Christ Church," the Church should support it financially until it could begin to grow again. The philosophical differences between the two men were irreconcilable, and at the end of Maynard's first year, Bray submitted his resignation.

Bray's resignation was regrettable to many who knew of his devotion to the School. "Canon Bray has done a fine job in developing the academic excellence of the School, and he is to be commended for his hard work and efforts in that regard," one board member said. In 1992 the board established the Canon Allen F. Bray Memorial Scholarship for Students of Color to preserve a legacy of fairness.

Father Carson with his granddaughter, Katherine Vaughan '93, at her graduation.

BENJAMIN M. CRABTREE
(HEADMASTER, 1981–88)

Headmaster Ben Crabtree at his desk, pen in one hand, ever-present pipe in the other.

The Vestry named Upper School Director Benjamin M. Crabtree Interim Headmaster beginning May 31, 1981. The former biology teacher and assistant football coach proved from the start that he had a competent and popular leadership style. **Robin Byrd** replaced Crabtree as Upper School Director and College Counselor, Ball remained Middle School Director, and Howard continued as Lower School Director.

By November Crabtree began making changes to address the lean enrollment. He wrote a report to the board with three recommendations. He stated that part of the enrollment troubles stemmed from children with mild to moderate learning disabilities whose families felt compelled to withdraw. He believed a program to serve these students would be beneficial. Crabtree also recommended initiating a Summer Academic Enrichment Program open to the whole community to enable more families to learn about CCES and see the campus. Finally, he asked for a business manager to handle finances and manage the physical plant.

Meanwhile, Maynard established his own short and long-term goals. He, like Crabtree, "thought the School was at a critical junction." We knew "it was time…to think long-term for both Parish and School," Maynard said.

Among the short-term goals was to improve of the appearance of the Lower School. Secondly, Maynard proposed expanding the Church's Mother's Morning Out program into a licensed preschool that would naturally feed into CCES. Thirdly, he hosted an annual Christmas party for the faculty at the parish rectory to show his appreciation for them.

Maynard also supported a Vestry movement to abolish the School Enrollment Certificates (See page 52). They had become burdensome to existing parents and discouraging to prospective families. Additionally, he hired **The Reverend Gil Dent** to assist with Church services and to act as Director of Development and Alumni Relations. Dent stayed from 1981–83, long enough to establish the Alumni Christmas Party and to start an annual fund.

In 1983 Crabtree introduced a foreign language program in grades 1–4 where Advanced Placement foreign language students in the Upper School taught introductory French, Spanish, and Latin in the Lower School. This short-lived program gave older students practice with their language skills and allowed for a part-time instructor. Another innovation was the addition of ten Apple IIe computers to each campus, made possible by the generosity of the Parents Organization.

Under Crabtree, the first CCES *News & Hi-Lites* was published to avoid "duplicate mailings" and "provide a publication suitable for public relations purposes." (Crabtree, *News & Hi-Lites*, April 1983) He also hired **Karen Abrams** as Development Director to manage fundraising and to input records into the computer system.

David R. Williams replaced Howard as Lower School Director in 1983. Among his lasting contributions was his work with the Greenville Speech Hearing & Learning Center to develop "a screening instrument for evaluating young children's potential." He said, "The information gleaned from the screenings enabled us to intentionally teach to the individual child, reducing failure and frustration." Today, the Speech Hearing & Learning Center continues to provide testing services for admission purposes.

Robin Byrd left CCES in 1985 and was replaced by **William (Bill) S. Dingledine, Jr.** (1985–97). Dingledine had most recently worked as Director of College Placement and Director of Admissions at Boys' Latin, an independent school in Baltimore, Maryland, with a philosophy similar to that of CCES. Experience as a football, wrestling, and lacrosse coach as well as a math and science teacher made him a valuable administrator.

Crabtree worked to improve the campus in his last years as Headmaster. With financial backing from the Parents Organization, the Athletic Booster Club, and individuals such as **Dexter Hagy** and **B. O. Thomason**, he was able to accomplish much. From 1986 to 1988, CCES acquired two school vans, a new track complex, five new athletic fields for girls' sports, a scoreboard for five new tennis courts, and a foreign language laboratory. In addition, Crabtree finished Phase I of a larger landscaping plan.

Like many faculty members, Crabtree had children at the School, and his personal and professional lives were hardly separate. He was a constant advocate for his teachers, and they in turn were a devoted group, despite little to no salary increases.

This photo from the early 80s shows Robin Byrd, Director of the Upper School, Headmaster Ben Crabtree, and Monte Ball, first Director of the Middle School.

> *The 80s were the halcyon days – test scores were high, top athletes were bringing home the crown. The National Merit Scholar Semifinalists, and National Merit Commended Scholar recipients were extraordinary. It was a time of high productivity – all on a very tight budget where the faculty had to "make do." It was a time of camaraderie, of warmth and informality between the faculty and students.*
>
> **—Diana Stafford (1974–2004)**

Crabtree left CCES in 1988 for a Headmaster position in North Carolina. Upon his departure, there were 603 students registered at CCES for the following year, indicating a possible upward trend in enrollment. Although he was not ever able to establish a specific program to address different learning styles, Crabtree's initial instincts were eventually proven correct. In 1996 CCES hired **Lee Churchill** as Head of Academic Resources.

JAMES (JIM) KEITH RUMRILL (HEADMASTER, 1988–97)

James (Jim) Keith Rumrill became Interim Headmaster of CCES effective July 1, 1988. Initially hired to calm the waters between Church and School and to reinvigorate School operations, he was invited to assume the permanent appointment in his second year. A retired U.S. Navy captain, Rumrill had lived and traveled in Europe. With degrees from the University of Florida, including a master's in international relations, he brought a global perspective and an emphasis on community outreach to CCES.

Previously Rumrill had served as teacher-coach, department head, principal, and assistant headmaster at Porter-Gaud School in Charleston, where he spearheaded integration and introduced co-education; then as Headmaster of The Catawba School in Rock Hill; then as Headmaster of Asheville Country Day School, which he merged with St. Genevieve-Gibbons Hall to become Carolina Day School. By all accounts, he had the experience to steer CCES into a broader, more secure future in the community.

As with any administration, there were challenges from the beginning. But with the aid of an industrious School Board, Rumrill had the ability to address most of them quickly. **James (Jim) B. Pressly, Jr.**, School Board Chair 1988–90, engineered a broad structure in which he named committees for specific issues. Then he wrote to the whole "School family" asking for their participation too. "We hope to utilize the talents available in our School family as fully as possible," he said. While this leadership approach was not altogether new, it was very effective in allowing Rumrill to spend more time on efforts to increase enrollment.

Almost immediately, Rumrill began to look for ways to broaden the reputation of the School in the community. Believing that a relationship with the changing Greenville business community would be mutually beneficial, he reached outward for financial support and to build enrollment. To this end, he tried some new approaches to

Although Headmaster Jim Rumrill spent much of his time promoting the School to the business community, he remained accessible to his devoted faculty and student body.

marketing, such as offering campus tours to real estate companies. He also became actively involved in Rotary, the Chamber of Commerce, the Literacy Association, the Urban League, and the Japan-America Association.

In April 1989 Rumrill oversaw a five-year self-study that the faculty and staff conducted for the Southern Association of Colleges and Schools (SACS) to determine how well CCES was serving its students, parents, and the community. It was a valuable tool in determining how to help the School grow. In late June, **Dale Bullen** moved that the board offer Rumrill the Headmaster position.

In the meantime, Maynard had begun to adopt what he called a "rector-friendly" manner of leadership. He advocated a strong relationship between the Church and School, but confessed to limited time to give to both. In an article for the National Association of Episcopal Schools (NAES), Maynard wrote:

> *Even if a Rector were so inclined, most would find the demands placed on them by their several parochial responsibilities too great to allow them to be involved in the day-to-day operations of the school.… The fact that the overwhelming majority of the students and alumni in a parish school will not be members of the Rector's parish adds still another dimension to the Rector's relationship to the school.*

Thus, Maynard became more of a figurehead at the School. He appeared at events to deliver speeches. He hosted faculty appreciation days, and he wrote articles promoting the School in parish and School publications. His ultimate authority over the board remained as it always had been, but his involvement in running the School lessened increasingly until his departure.

In April 1990, as part of Rumrill's initiative to reach out to the Greenville business community, the Board of Visitors, a group of informed and enthusiastic ambassadors for CCES, met for the first time. Their mission was to complement the work of the School Board. **Langhorne (Lanny) T. Webster** was highly instrumental in helping Rumrill recruit many of Greenville's most respected business leaders for the board. (See page 142 for a list of the Board of Visitors charter members.) The board was chaired by **Dr. Gordon W. Blackwell**, retired President of Furman University, and co-chaired by **C. Langdon Cheves, Jr.** To bring the school community closer together, he also asked the board to approve two additional charter organizations: the Gold Cavaliers for former faculty, and the Cavalier Classics, for parents of alumni.

As the new marketing efforts bore fruit and enrollment started to increase, the question of whether to consolidate the Lower, Middle, and Upper Schools onto one campus bubbled beneath the surface. School Board Chair **Robert (Bob) E. Hughes** requested an in-depth study on the matter. Perry Earle, Chairman of the Task Force, concluded that such a move

would be "advantageous to both the Church and the School if the Church really must have more space and if the School can increase the size of the student body." Earle insisted, however, "The one prerequisite is a capital campaign that can raise enough money to pay for the cost of constructing and furnishing new facilities on the Cavalier Campus."

Enrollment climbed to 697 by the fall of 1992, yielding an unexpected budget surplus, and all enrollment certificates were retired. The School was finally in a good position to address the crowding in the Lower School. Many months passed, however, before a temporary solution came to light. Upper School Director Bill Dingledine suggested adding a classroom, wrestling and weight training wing onto the McCall Field House, which would also temporarily hold fifth and sixth grades. The idea appealed to the practical-minded board. By the fall of 1993 the new wing became a reality through the efforts of architects Craig Gaulden Davis, board member **Lang Donkle '67**, and Middle School Director **John Walter '77**.

In February 1994, School Board Chair **Pat Haskell-Robinson** announced construction would begin in the summer on a permanent Middle School building and dining facilities. In the spring, after Freeman & Major Architects completed their drawings, a "Campaign for Excellence" was launched to fund the work. One significant gift was a charitable donation by The Wenwood Investment Company of 17.64 acres of land off Wenwood Road.

> *One of my fond memories of this period [is] meeting in **Frank Halter's** office to review the plat of that piece of property and seeing how he masterfully worked out a deal with the Wenwood Partners to donate the entire piece to the school.*
>
> —Jim Rumrill

Rector Dennis Maynard and Headmaster Jim Rumrill outside the Lower School downtown.

In the midst of fundraising and construction, Rumrill set goals pertaining to the curriculum and athletic program in connection with the SACS study, and he put diversity at the forefront of the long-range plan for the School. With the opening of the BMW plant in 1994, which brought a large new international community to Greenville, he knew CCES needed to recognize and embrace the demographic changes taking place in the Upstate.

To this end, Rumrill began an English as a Second Language Program (ESL) for students in grades 5–12. He, along with John Walter, established exchange programs in Japan and Holland. **Mrs. Toshiko Kishimoto**, principal of the Japanese Saturday School, joined the faculty as consultant for Asian students. In addition, Rumrill asked **Gerald Protheroe**, History Department Chair, to attend the International Baccalaureate (IB) program in Wales.

In February 1995 Dennis Maynard left the parish as Rector. Upon his departure, **The Reverend Stephen Williams** and **The Reverend Burke S. Stathers, Jr.,** who served as Interim Rector, took on more responsibilities while a committee searched for Maynard's replacement. Extraordinary growth had occurred in both Church and School during Maynard's fifteen years of service. Although this expansion was due in part to a stronger economy, those at the top were clearly instrumental in nurturing the growth.

The new Middle School building was ready for occupancy by the start of the 1995–96 school year. Total enrollment had now climbed to 875 students, and all Middle and Lower School classes were full. For most, it was the beginning of a promising era. However, two much loved and dedicated leaders decided it was time to step aside. Bill Dingledine announced his resignation after ten years. **James C. Carbaugh**, founder and Director of the International Baccalaureate (IB) Program at Southside High School in Greenville, became Upper School Director the following fall.

Rumrill also announced his retirement, with a year's notice to allow "for an orderly transition," he said. The following day, School Board Chair **Julius (Gil) A. Gilreath, Jr.**, wrote to the CCES family of Rumrill's decision with "a great deal of sadness." Students and faculty were equally heavy-hearted at his departure. Although he, more than any Headmaster before him, had looked outward for School support, Rumrill had stayed closely involved with his students and staff. "Mr. Rumrill was always very tender," recalled **Katherine Russell Sagedy '89**. "I was a senior when he came. Mr. Rumrill [was] very distinguished; he [had] that fatherly demeanor. That's what I remember most."

In appreciation, the board named Rumrill *Headmaster Emeritus* and established a scholarship endowment for faculty/staff children in his name.

ELLEN Y. MOCERI
(HEAD OF SCHOOL, 1997–2000)

The Church and the School found themselves simultaneously conducting searches for a new Headmaster and a new Church Rector. **Sallie P. White** and **Francis DeLoache Ellison '68** co-chaired the Search Committee for a new Head of School. Rather than rely solely on "word of mouth" recommendations, they hired a consulting firm in Boston to broaden the search. Here was an opportunity to carefully consider the direction of the School as it moved into the next century. The committee traveled to Atlanta twice to narrow the large number of applicants for more interviews in Greenville.

Among the finalists was Ellen Y. Moceri, who stood out as having a philosophy that aligned with that of CCES. In November 1996, Moceri wrote to the committee:

> *I am an Episcopalian and profoundly committed to the role that our schools must play in the ethical and character development of our students. I share your commitment to developing the full potential of our children, not only in academic excellence, but also in the arts, athletics and community service. In preparing our students to face the challenges of the 21st century, we need to help them acquire a global perspective – one that helps them realize their potential as global citizens. Christ Church School's commitment to diversity helps further that aim.*

Head of School Ellen Moceri introduced the International Baccalaureate programs to increase the level of academic rigor in the curriculum and to emphasize a commitment to global education.

In February 1997 the board named Moceri "Head of School." Her resumé of twenty-five years at John Burroughs School in St. Louis, Missouri, and later as Head of Upper School at Horace Mann School in Riverdale, New York, signaled that she had the experience to lead CCES forward.

The search for a new Rector ended at nearly the same time. Two months after hiring Moceri, the board introduced The Reverend Dr. Robert (Bob) S. Dannals (Rector, 1997–2007) at the April meeting. Dannals had most recently served as Rector of Trinity Church in Statesville, North Carolina, and Christ Church in New Bern, North Carolina.

Moceri arrived from New York on July 1, 1997. Within a short time, she had written to the parents, students, faculty, and staff of developments that portended a "rigorous and challenging year." Among them was the formation of a chaplaincy team, including **The Reverend John Pollock** and lay chaplains **Joseph (Joe) E. Britt** and **Valerie Morris Riddle**, who would oversee the Upper, Middle, and Lower Schools respectively. The second change was that all buildings would have access to the Internet as well as e-mail capability at the start of the year. Junior and senior students would have e-mail accounts, connecting them to the larger world.

In October, after having visited the Davidson International Baccalaureate (IB) Middle School in Charlotte, Moceri extolled the merits of the IB curriculum to the board. She said it was "the up-and-coming curriculum recognized by the very finest institutions in the United States." Its virtue was that it was "a connected curriculum" in contrast to the Advanced Placement (AP) curriculum. International standards would also validate the excellence of the School's teaching.

A subcommittee of the board's Education Committee agreed to investigate the IB program further. Key to the investigation were reports from the Lower, Middle, and Upper School directors on how it would change the existing curriculum. Faculty from all grades then visited other independent schools already immersed in the IB program, and returned with mostly favorable reports.

Dannals, among others, voiced reservation. He feared that because Christian education was not part of the IB curriculum, there would need to be an "intentional and collaborative effort, as well as tremendous discipline by the faculty at all levels of the school" to ensure that this founding principle would not be compromised in any way.

Adding to the atmosphere of debate was another sensitive topic. With the Church in need of more space, Moceri, Sallie White, faculty member **Emmy Holt**, and **Robert (Tex) S. Small, Jr.,** approached the executive council of the Vestry about moving the Lower School to Cavalier Drive. They knew the move would be costly and controversial.

Rector Bob Dannals and Head of School Ellen
Moceri both came to the School in 1997.

Fortunately, the debate was short-lived. In March 1998 White read a letter by **Julian Dority**, Vestry representative to the board, saying, "On February 14, 1998, the Vestry of Christ Church Episcopal approved the following motion: I hereby move that the Vestry of Christ Church Episcopal endorse and approve that all three divisions of Christ Church Episcopal School be located at the Cavalier Campus subject to the Church and its bylaws." Applause followed the reading that validated the decision.

At the same March meeting, the board voted unanimously to approve the IB program for grades Primer to 12. "We need a curriculum that will add coherence to our school," Holt said in her report. "The IB curriculum would give CCES the opportunity to make learning more global, more relevant, and more fun," she added.

In July 1998 Lower School Director **Becky Brown** announced that she had accepted a position in Atlanta. Her departure meant the end of ten years of talented service to CCES. **Denise R. Pearsall** was appointed as Brown's replacement. She had taught in the Lower School for seven years and had been selected in the inaugural group of recipients of the Daniel-Mickel Foundation Master Teacher Award before moving into administrative roles as Assistant Director of the Lower School and Director of Admissions.

In January 1999 Upper School Director Chris Carbaugh took an appointment as Academic Director of South Carolina Governor's School for the Arts and Humanities. He had been instrumental in the long process of obtaining IB authorization. **Dr. Vincent M. Stumpo** arrived in June 1999 to replace Carbaugh. He had a degree in physics and chemistry from St. Joseph's University, a PhD in physical chemistry from the University of Delaware, and a well-defined idea of independent education that resonated with Moceri's.

In August Moceri held her third board retreat at the Hyatt. Lanny Webster, chair of the board's Development Committee, had become a powerful force on the board with a reputation for cultivating support in the community. Her dedication stemmed from a long association with the School, first as the mother of two graduates, and then as a board member during three administrations, including Bethea's, Bray's, and Rumrill's. Now she was serving a third term to help raise the necessary funds for a consolidated campus.

To many, it looked as if the next nine months would be abundantly productive. Board Chair Tex Small made a family commitment of $1 million toward the capital campaign. He also indicated that the Cavalier Campus Master Plan would be ready for the September meeting. Moceri set goals to increase salary compensation and endowment, and all division heads were committed to implementing the IB program.

But discontent began to surface among parents and alumni. In less than three years, a sizable transformation had occurred at the School, in terms of curriculum, personnel changes, and vision for the campus. These changes upset the balance between tradition and progress, and a divide arose among those in favor of Moceri and those who doubted her direction.

Moceri made numerous efforts to diffuse the mounting tensions throughout the following months. During Convocation and at Middle and Upper School chapel services, she spoke of the virtue of overcoming difficulty. But by February 2000 it was apparent that the spirit of cooperation that had existed during Moceri's first two years had dissolved. There was little doubt that many important changes had taken place, but there was sufficient unrest in the School and the community for the board to allow Moceri to be released from her contract at the end of the year.

Moceri remained Head of School until the end of June. To her credit and that of Dannals, the Vestry, and the School Board, civility prevailed among the fractured leadership, and both the capital campaign and campus changes initiated by Moceri continued at a surprising rate. She, along with Small, Stumpo, and CCES Business Manager **David J. Matthewson**, formed a Planning Committee for a new Upper School. They visited schools that had undergone recent construction, noting the best features of each. Moceri said it was essential to build a high school for the twenty-first century—"full of appropriate technology and spaces for interactive teaching." Plans also began to take shape for transforming the existing Upper School building to meet the needs of a relocated Lower School.

In more than two decades at CCES, Denise Pearsall moved from the classroom to administration. As Lower School Director, she presided over the move from downtown to the Cavalier Campus and embraced the IB Primary Years Program enthusiastically.

In her remarks on Awards Night, Moceri spoke of overwhelming pride in the graduating class, whom she credited with raising "the academic standards of the School." It was a bittersweet departure for her. Although the atmosphere now called for new leadership, there was no mistaking that Moceri had provided direction to CCES at an important crossroad.

DR. LELAND H. COX, JR.
(HEADMASTER, 2000–10)

The search for a new Headmaster ended when the board voted unanimously to appoint Dr. Leland (Lee) H. Cox, Jr., as Headmaster effective July 1, 2000. He had spent thirteen years as Founding President of the South Carolina Governor's School for Science and Mathematics in Hartsville and another thirteen years as Executive Director of the South Carolina Humanities Council. Not only was his background impressive, but he also had the reputation of being a facilitator, negotiator, and problem-solver.

William (Bill) C. Sparrgrove, from St. Stephen's Episcopal School in Florida, replaced Stumpo as Upper School Director a month later. With teaching and administrative experience at schools both in the U.S. and abroad, he would guide the upper grades through transition to the new IB curriculum. Both Cox and Sparrgrove faced immediate challenges, not the least of which was implementing the IB program, constructing a high school building, and completing a capital campaign.

With the implementation of the IB programs, Cox placed a high priority on cultivation of the international community at CCES. He concurred with Rumrill's and Moceri's beliefs that global awareness was important to the education of all students in the twenty-first century. Cox and Sparrgrove met regularly with representatives from BMW to discuss issues, such as the School's foreign language program, that would impact German students. He also engaged in discussions with members of the Michelin School, and he broadened the international training of the faculty by investing heavily in IB training—a move that energized many faculty

Headmaster Lee Cox presided over the consolidation of the Cavalier Campus and the building of the Chapel of the Good Shepherd.

members—and by sending representatives from each School division to visit Santiago College, a K-12 IB school in Santiago, Chile.

In the meantime, the Governance Task Force Committee of the School Board began to actively address the issue of separating the Church and the now mature School. Up to this point and in accordance with the bylaws, the Church had maintained final authority over the School. All employment contracts were still signed by the Rector, and the Church held all the School's endowment funds. But significant growth in both the Church and the School had made this management arrangement impractical. So with the blessings of both Board Chair Gil Gilreath and Rector Dannals, legal proceedings began to incorporate the School as a separate 501c(3) non-profit entity.

At first, it was unclear the degree to which the two bodies would operate apart from one another. Compounding concerns was the impending move of the Lower School to the Cavalier Campus. Questions arose about the very identity of CCES if it were less tightly linked to Christ Church.

Commencement ceremonies have been steeped in tradition since the first one in 1972. An innovation introduced by Lee Cox was having the faculty dress in academic robes. Here, they line up to applaud the new graduates.

Dannals's voice of reason prevailed throughout long discussions on the change. He calmed emotions by saying that the name, Christ Church Episcopal School, obligated the School to remain under "the appropriate and applicable canons of the Episcopal Church and the authority of the Bishop." He added, "We are still an Episcopal School in every way." Board member Artie McCall endorsed the move, saying it was a necessary step for both institutions, and on April 26, 2001, CCES officially became incorporated separately from the Church.

While governance issues were being resolved, the School moved ahead with a third major capital campaign. In 1999 "One, Together" Capital Campaign co-chairs, **Ralph (Mickey) Wilson Callahan, Jr.,** and Tex Small, Development Director **Connie B. Lanzl**, and the board had set a goal of $13 million to build a new Upper School, renovate the old building for the Lower School, construct a chapel, and double the endowment.

Students moved into the new Upper School in January 2002. Later, in May, under the guidance of Frances Ellison and with recommendations from Cox, the board adopted a new strategic plan. Completion of the Lower School by the fall and construction of a chapel were among the primary objectives. The challenge lay in raising the money to pay for these buildings. Enrollment was at a healthy 970, just short of the targeted 980, but tuition alone could not produce revenue for these projects.

In time for the start of the 2002–03 school year, the Lower School relocated to the Cavalier Campus, bringing all students together in one location for the first time since 1970. The campus—as originally imagined by Arthur McCall, Sr.—looked as if it would be complete at last. Attention now turned to the need for a chapel. Parishioner and former board member Frank B. Halter agreed to chair the Chapel Committee.

The gift that gave certainty to construction of the chapel came, ironically, from a childless couple with a desire to "remember the community in a special way." In December 2003 **Dr. Francis Thompson Smith**, a friend of board member **Edgar M. Norris, Jr.**, pledged the first of several gifts in honor of his deceased wife, **Martha**. The $1.5 million that he ultimately gave to the "One, Together" campaign comprised the largest gift in the School's history.

Charles C. (Charlie) Mickel, Chair of the Chapel Design Committee, monitored construction of the chapel until it was completed in September 2005. His commitment to the project was critical. Mickel and his brother, **Buck, Jr.**, had been students at CCES beginning in 1967. Their sister, **Minor Mickel Shaw**, had sent her children to the School in the 90s. Now Charlie's children would benefit from their father's stewardship. Their parents, **Buck** and **Minor Mickel, Sr.**, had been loyal and supportive friends to CCES throughout its long history.

Sun streamed through rich and colorful stained glass as the Chapel of the Good Shepherd was consecrated by **The Right Reverend Dorsey F. Henderson, Jr.**, in a series of services on September 8 and 9, 2005. There was a celebratory mood on campus. The original vision for the School was now complete.

At nearly the same time, Cox announced a restructuring of the administration. Cox put management in the hands of his senior administrators, including Assistant Headmaster Bill Sparrgrove, Business Manager **William (Bill) Preston**, Development Director Connie Lanzl, Senior Chaplain **Richard B. Grimball**, **Jr.**, and Athletic Director **Ashley G. Haskins**. The shift freed him to concentrate on "development, fundraising, endowment, and cultivation."

A subsequent administrative change came with the creation of a new position, Associate Headmaster, whose responsibility was to manage the academic side of the School and to oversee and coordinate the efforts of the three division directors. **Dr. Leonard Kupersmith**, former Headmaster of Thomas Jefferson Independent Day School in Joplin, Missouri, was appointed Interim Associate Headmaster for the 2006–07 year. He quickly proved himself as an administrator, and the interim year led to a permanent assignment. **Valerie (Val) E. Hendrickson**, parent of two CCES graduates and former Assistant Middle School Director, replaced Walter as Director of the Middle School. A year later, **Peter (Pete) D. Sanders** replaced Sparrgrove as Upper School Director, and **Wesley (Wes) Clarke** became Dean of Students for the Upper School, a redefined position with responsibility for course scheduling, monitoring academic progress, student activities, and disciplinary issues.

In 2008 Board Chair Norris engineered another significant change in the administrative structure. Cox was given the title of President, a move designed to highlight his responsibilities in fundraising, strategic planning, and finance. Kupersmith was named Headmaster, charged with management of the divisions, athletics, and admission.

Fifty years have passed since Arthur McCall met with a few resolute parents in search of a better place to educate their children. Some of these people are deceased now, including the elder McCall. Others still act as champions for the dream they helped birth. Today, Christ Church Episcopal School is the sum product of dedicated leaders and builders, courageous decisions, and unyielding determination to be the best school possible.

Lee Cox became the School's first President in 2008.

The Landscape of Learning

From the beginning there was a vision for the place that was to become Christ Church Episcopal School. But could its founders have imagined the seventy-two-acre Cavalier Campus that fifty years later would serve more than one thousand students in half a dozen buildings? Can we envision the CCES of 2059? Probably not. The journey to this place has been one of continual growth and maturity. Certainly there have been bumps along the road, but, together, the School community has endured them with grace, humor, and generosity. The result has been a place of learning that is ever-changing but always grounded in its core values.

CHAPTER

3

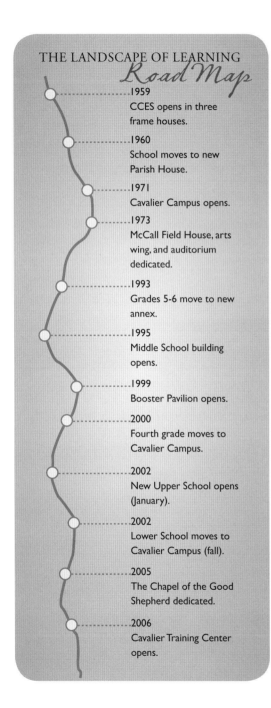

THE LANDSCAPE OF LEARNING
Road Map

1959
CCES opens in three frame houses.

1960
School moves to new Parish House.

1971
Cavalier Campus opens.

1973
McCall Field House, arts wing, and auditorium dedicated.

1993
Grades 5-6 move to new annex.

1995
Middle School building opens.

1999
Booster Pavilion opens.

2000
Fourth grade moves to Cavalier Campus.

2002
New Upper School opens (January).

2002
Lower School moves to Cavalier Campus (fall).

2005
The Chapel of the Good Shepherd dedicated.

2006
Cavalier Training Center opens.

When you look at the verdant Cavalier Campus today, it is hard to picture the scraggly pines and brown underbrush that once covered the landscape. It is even difficult to imagine a time when that campus consisted of one lone brick building seemingly in the middle of nowhere.

Today the CCES campus encompasses six major buildings, five athletic fields, and five tennis courts on 72.87 acres of land between Mauldin Road and Fairforest. It is accessible to students who drive from Travelers Rest, Simpsonville, Laurens, and Anderson, and it is roughly fifteen minutes from most in-town neighborhoods. It is a thriving hub of activity that has evolved over fifty years through the generosity and foresight of many.

The School began in three wood frame houses, now long vanished. Soon afterward it expanded to grade 9, and moved to a new Church Parish House. Although there had long been a desire to add a high school to complete the burgeoning school, it was not until 1968 when impetus for this goal became a possibility. Only when Jean McKissick offered her Crescent Avenue home for the express purpose of establishing a high school did a new campus become possible.

The search for the right site required persistence on the part of the Vestry committee assigned to the task. Several properties were flawed upon close examination. Then one particular site emerged as a real possibility. Perry Earle knew a group of investors known as Wenwood Associates who owned a large tract of land off Mauldin Road. They were all Church members, including **Walter Griffin Jr.**, **Robert S. Small, Sr.**, **Francis M. Hipp**, **J. Kelly Sisk**, and **Charles Ballenger**, and they were assisted by the professional services of Frank Halter and **C. Thomas (Tommy) Wyche**. Earle approached them with an offer in which the sellers would donate an acre of land for every acre bought. The Wenwood group agreed to the offer, in part because they knew that a school campus would positively impact the surrounding undeveloped land.

The property out there was completely unoccupied at that time. There were no units or industrial sites or anything. We walked all over it, every inch of it. We kept looking all over town and found that this was the best place to go. It was ideal in that it was big enough, adjacent to the population and large enough to expand.

—Perry Earle

Once the land was secure, a movement to raise money for construction began. The Church had just concluded a capital fund drive for $1 million in 1968, so it took some work to generate enthusiasm for another campaign. Even so, parishioners found a way to fulfill the dream.

The money that was raised came almost entirely from people at Christ Church – almost every cent of it. Perry came up with an idea that some people liked and some didn't, but it worked. For a long time, every student had to buy an enrollment certificate to be admitted. With some donations and the loan from mortgaging the Wenwood property, we were able to build the high school.

—Randolph Stone

Craig Gaulden Davis Architects submitted a progressive schematic study for the Upper School building that emphasized large, open spaces to encourage independence and creativity. It was conceptually very different from the Parish House, where the small, traditional classrooms doubled as Sunday School rooms.

"The building will be quite flexible, providing space not only for conventional classes, but also having facilities whereby a large number of students may work independently," Rufus Bethea told curious parents. "Also included in the plans are more space per student, comfortably furnished, carpeted, and air-conditioned rooms, and the latest in instructional materials."

Neither pouring rain on moving day in October 1971 nor unassembled carrels nor late deliveries could quell students' enthusiasm for finally settling into their own building, even if the design was surprising.

Charles Runge '84 on the Upper School payphone. If a student forgot lunch or a textbook at home, it was the only way to call home.

Laura Tate '86 and Christine Dixon '86 strike a pose atop the original sign marking the entrance to the Cavalier Campus.

THE "DREADED" ENROLLMENT *Certificates*

In 1973 the Upper School building still smelled of fresh paint and new carpet when the Board of Trustees decided to move forward with a second building phase. It included a field house, an arts wing, and an auditorium that would complete plans for the Cavalier Campus. While enthusiasm for more construction was abundant, the source of revenue was less obvious.

"Due to the two major capital fund drives [the Church in 1968 for $1 million and the School in 1970 for $1.7 million] we had to devise a way to fund the auditorium and field house," Father Carson said. "We came up with the dreaded bonds. We called them 'enrollment certificates.' The idea was that hopefully parents would give them to us when their children graduated. Didn't always work out."

A twenty-three-page document required parents to pay $1,500 for the first child they enrolled and $1,000 for the second. "Rather than increase tuition, which is now earmarked for current operating costs, the School has chosen to require the purchase of Enrollment Certificates so that future students, as well as present ones, will bear a proportionate share of the cost of the current building program," one explanation read. They could redeem the bonds at graduation for face value, but they had to turn around and sell them to an incoming parent.

Brilliant though the plan was in terms of paying for the construction of the field house and the auditorium, it did not evolve into a reliable source of income. In the end, most parents chose to be reimbursed. By the early 80s, enrollment had begun to decline and the certificates were a deterrent to potential young families. The School Board recommended to the Vestry that there be a one-time, nonrefundable enrollment fee of $500 to replace the bonds.

"The fee would be used to slowly work off the $1,500-$2,500 building certificates that were still outstanding even though it would take a longer period of time to do so," said Artie McCall (School Board 1982–85, 1998–2002). "… The end result was that enrollment began to increase, the School became more financially viable, and the ones who wanted their certificates redeemed all received their money."

Somehow this conservative group of minds had consented to a building plan that lacked interior walls. It was called an "open" plan. Most of the students assumed they ran out of money before the walls could be built. In the center of this open space was the "library," which had some books but definitely was not quiet since it was the only way to get to the other side of the building (unless of course you wanted to walk past the Headmaster's office – not a popular route).
—Sally Casteel Craven '75

On March 22, 1973, students and faculty assembled as **The Right Reverend George M. Alexander**, Arthur McCall, Perry Earle, and Student Council President **Alfred Robinson '73** broke ground for a second phase of construction at the Cavalier Campus. This phase included space for the arts and athletic programs.

The completion phase (Phase II) includes, among other things, an oversized field house. The building will be the first in the Greenville area with a composition floor that will allow for a multi-sports program indoors. Included in another building will be a 500-seat theater, dining facilities, typing room, music studio, art studio, shop and various other small room needs.
—Rufus Bethea

THE GROUNDS

Once Phase II was complete, the grounds around the buildings took priority. Funds were limited and resources were scarce because of the recent construction, so parents, faculty, and students stepped up to the challenge of improving and maintaining the landscape. They had a vested interest in making the School look its best.

The Booster Club, which started in 1972 "to boost morale among the athletic teams," found big and small ways to improve the athletic facilities, even with modest financial contributions. They took responsibility for such things as carpet and a trophy cabinet in the McCall Field House in the 70s, maintaining the track in the mid-80s, and resurfacing the tennis courts in the 90s.

Today the Booster Club has a membership of over 220 families that raises more than $35,000 annually. It is an essential part of the growing athletic program. Most recently, it sponsored the CCES Booster Pavilion in 1999 and the Cavalier Training Center in 2006. It also contributes to the upkeep of the gymnasium and the athletic fields.

The Parents Organization, which was created in 1971 to generate communication between the parents and the School, added to the spirit of involvement. It quickly became an effective vehicle for rallying parents behind different projects and needs. In 1976 it organized the first annual Super Saturday, a spring festival for the entire family that helped supplement the general operating fund.

Over the course of fifty years, there were also certain individuals who devoted exceptional amounts of time and energy to improving the campus. These especially dedicated and often unrecognized people, some of whom were teachers, have left a legacy that is hard to quantify.

Spring is heralded on campus by the flowering cherry trees, a gift from the Class of 1988.

School spirit rocks Carson Stadium. Here, during 2004 Homecoming festivities, a girls powder puff team cheers classmates on the field.

Thanks to the McCall Endowment, Artie and George McCall, and the Booster Club, the McCall Field House received a facelift in 2006 with a new wood floor, fresh paint, and cleaned championship banners.

"McCall Field House wasn't complete when we moved to the Cavalier Campus," noted **Coach Jim Tate** (1969–76). "So we hauled in 18-wheel tractor-trailers to use as team dressing rooms. The fields were not much more than pasture at the time. Perry Earle loaned us a tractor, and a lot of committed parents, including Rufus Bethea's entire family, worked long hours transforming the pastures into athletic fields."

In 1976 **Bob Hassold**, **Tom Hipp**, and **David Quattlebaum**, all of whom were board members at the time, manually built creosote steps into the red clay bank leading to the tennis courts and down to the hockey field. Much to the pride of the "Hammer Team" as they called themselves, the faded and cracked wooden stairs remained in place until 2007 when the School finally replaced them with concrete steps.

In the early 90s, attorney **Bob Ariail**, father of **Mills '91** and **Brooks '94**, came to the School after work to water, cut, and fertilize the fields. "He spent countless hours because he wanted my sister and me to have the best fields in the state to play on," said Mills. "I remember him sodding the entire baseball field! I truly believe that CCES has the great fields it does today because my dad put his heart and soul into that job."

Shown under construction in 1994, the Middle School was the first major building to be added to the Cavalier Campus since the McCall Field House in 1973.

A NEW MIDDLE SCHOOL

If the 70s and 80s were the decades during which the focus became the fields and grounds, then the mid-90s could be considered the start of a second major building phase.

When I think of CCES in the mid-90s, I think of change. This is the time in the School's history when we truly became introspective. Are we doing a good job? Who are our customers? Are we satisfying these customers? What does it take to maintain and improve our faculty? What about our facilities? What do we need to do to become a first-class learning institution not only for today but also for the future? The latter part of the 90s [was] the School's aggressive response to the questions posed.

—Gil Gilreath, School Board Chair 1995–97, 2000–01

In 1993 the administration turned its attention to building a Middle School. Again, the motivation was to have a suitable facility for this unique age group. Based on reputable programs around the country, there was growing consensus that the "middle years" had become grades 5–8, rather than just 7–8.

While the Middle School was being planned and constructed, fifth and sixth grades moved from the downtown campus to an annex of the field house. Here they stayed for the 1993–95 school years, happily cocooned and separate from the high school. Spanish teacher **Joy Baker** (1992–2008) recounted the transition from the Parish Campus:

> *Everything was taken from the 5th and 6th grade rooms and loaded onto one 18-wheeler. This was then parked behind the gym on the Cavalier Campus for the summer while construction on our new annex was finished.*
>
> *During that summer, **Mrs. [Sally] Henley** and **Mrs. [Ginny] Tate** were taking a course together. They needed to get some of Mrs. Tate's notes from a previous course, but of course the notes were packed in box #3 in the truck. Desperate, they unlocked the truck, but found the box right away!!*
>
> *We opened 5th and 6th grades in the fall of '93…Our rooms were so open and airy we thought we'd died and gone to heaven!! You could see out the windows! The windows opened and let in fresh air!! We didn't have to run through a graveyard to get to recess!! We had grassy fields and four-square and tennis courts for recess!! We had a cafeteria to get lunch in!!*
>
> *….How could life get any better? It did!! In the fall of 1995, we moved 5th and 6th into the top floor of the new Middle School building!!*

Middle School Director John Walter III with students at the grand opening of the new building.

Left, Before moving to the Cavalier Campus, the entire Lower School student body and faculty gathered for one last official picture. The graveyard through which students walked to reach the playground is in the background.

Above, On their last day on the Parish Campus, Lower School students chalked their goodbyes outdoors on the pavement and brick walls.

Left, Excited students waited to see President George W. Bush's motorcade as it drove by the downtown campus in 2001. The following year, the Lower School moved to the Cavalier Campus.

Left, The architecture of the Middle School gives students social as well as academic spaces.

Right, The founders' wisdom in providing ample acreage for the Cavalier Campus has become ever more apparent with the growth in enrollment and facilities in the 2000s. When the chapel was sited in the center of campus, a new playground was constructed behind the Middle School, and a memorial garden with a life-size bronze sculpture of Blair Babb Smoak was created behind the Upper School to replace the amphitheater named in her memory.

The Middle School opened in time for the 1995–96 year. Architect **Allen Freeman** of Freeman & Major Architects had designed a unique two-story, 43,000-square-foot, state-of-the-art facility with sixteen classrooms, four science laboratories, expanded space for fine arts, a library, administrative offices, and a commons area for each floor. The commons areas replaced hallways, allowing teachers to keep an unobtrusive eye on students as they moved between classes. There were also two dining rooms and a kitchen, which accommodated both Middle and Upper School students. More cause for celebration was the fact that the successful "Campaign for Excellence" left the School without construction debt and with funds for future maintenance.

The following summer, athletic fields again became a priority. A combined effort by the Booster Club and the School Board led to several significant changes: the baseball and softball fields switched places in order for the baseball field to become "a legitimate size for high school ball," the field hockey program took the soccer field as its own, and the soccer program gained practice fields, as well as the ability to use the football stadium for home matches.

Left, Headmaster Lee Cox, a licensed pilot, flew over the Cavalier Campus in 2000 to obtain aerial photos as the foundation was being laid for the new Upper School (*upper right*). By contrast, just ten years earlier in August 1990, the wooded campus consisted only of the Upper School, arts wing, McCall Field House, and several athletic fields.

Above, Wearing tee shirts proclaiming "The beautiful is difficult…TO MOVE," a riff on the School's motto, students and faculty rest after moving books and furnishings to the new Upper School.

Left, Sam Smith '82 on the Upper School construction site in 2000. His firm, Triangle Construction, also built the Middle School in 1994.

Chapter 3: *The Landscape of Learning*   59

Student Council President Kevin Roe '02, *center*, gets ready to cut the ribbon at opening ceremonies for the new Upper School. With him are, *from left*, Upper School Director Bill Sparrgrove, Ralph Callahan, Ingram Carpenter '06, Headmaster Lee Cox, Brooke Carpin '02, Frances Ellison, Tex Small, and Father Bob Dannals.

In February 1997 the Middle School installed playground equipment, thanks to the combined generosity of **Raoul** and **Susan Glenn**, the Booster Club, the Parents Organization, and the Middle School classes. There were more athletic improvements in 1998 due to donations from a CCES parent, **John Reed**, who supplemented Booster Club funds. The weight room received modern training equipment, new record boards, and a fresh coat of paint. The Reeds' support also enabled the resurfacing of the tennis courts in "Cavalier Blue," new lighting in Carson Stadium and on the baseball field and tennis courts, a new scoreboard on the Linda Reeves Hockey Field, and the yellow-topped fencing around the baseball field. In addition, CCES purchased three mini-buses and uniforms for almost every sports team.

FINALLY, ONE, TOGETHER

The excitement created by steady improvements to the Cavalier Campus was tempered, though, by the fact that the Lower School remained almost a school unto itself on Washington Street. Two campuses were no longer practical, so the idea to bring the Lower School to Cavalier Drive gradually gained appeal.

To accomplish this, co-chairs Ralph Callahan and Tex Small rallied support for the "One, Together" campaign that began in 1999. By the time the public phase was announced, over $8 million had already been raised. In addition to a new Upper School, campaign goals included renovating the old Upper School so it could become the Lower School by the fall of 2002, building a chapel, and increasing endowment. It was a lot to accomplish but the time seemed right to address multiple needs.

Construction began on the new three-story, 70,000-square-foot Upper School building in August 2000, shortly after Headmaster Lee Cox arrived on campus. Not until January 2002 did the Upper School students move into their new quarters. The wait was worthwhile because Allen Freeman had designed a facility that was spectacular in terms of appearance and function. It offered highly sophisticated science labs, expansive art studios, a spacious 7,500-square-foot library, and wiring for technology.

The new Upper School was designed with 66,000 square feet on three levels. Its features include a 7,500 square-foot library, four state-of-the-art science labs, two art studios, a darkroom, blackbox theater, and technology labs.

DR. FRANCIS THOMPSON SMITH'S *Gift*

Dr. Smith made his generous gift to the School in memory of his beloved wife Martha.

it was as if Smith had become part of a big family that needed him as much as he needed it during his last years. The mutual affection led to a financial gift that gave the project the financial backing and momentum needed to break ground. During the dedication of the chapel a frail Dr. Smith rose in his front-row seat to read these simple remarks:

I am so happy to make this gift. It was made in memory of my wife Martha. She would be delighted to be here with all of the students. I have enjoyed being a part of the Christ Church Episcopal School community where I have made many friends. I have especially enjoyed the letters, the visits, pictures, and e-mail from so many of you.

Edgar M. Norris, Jr., a CCES parent and member of the School Board during several administrations, introduced Dr. Francis Thompson Smith to Lee Cox following a conversation in which Smith asked Norris to advise him on what to do with his substantial savings. At first, Norris suggested Smith consider a gift to Christ Church, where Smith attended. The idea was attractive to Francis. But after Martha's death in 2002, another idea began to resonate with greater appeal. By this time, he had heard that Christ Church Episcopal School was trying to raise money for a campus chapel. As he became familiar with the School, he developed a deep affection for the place and its people. Visits by adoring and energetic students at his nursing home and a regular seat of honor at school performances all helped ease the loneliness of life without Martha. Since he had no children of his own,

Dr. Francis Smith became a familiar figure on campus, and the children at CCES became part of his extended family.

In February 2002 **The Right Reverend Dorsey F. Henderson, Jr.,** Bishop of Upper South Carolina, consecrated the handsome brick building in a reverent service from *The Book of Common Prayer*. He returned a few months later to bless the new Lower School building that opened later that fall. Although the liturgy was the same, the second service was far different from the solemn first. This time, the amused Bishop found himself being trailed by children who could barely contain their voices and who wanted blessings on every fixture in their school including bathrooms!

The Lower School was impressive in its own right. Architects **Michael Keeshen** and **Dan Waddell** of Michael Keeshen & Associates renovated the former high school building with both modern and traditional features. Gone were the large, shapeless spaces separated by less-than-soundproof dividers of the 70s and 80s. Gone, too, were the small, windowless classrooms of the Parish Campus, where teachers had to share their rooms with Sunday School classes. Instead, large, bright classrooms with commons areas skirted an enclosed and highly technical library.

The windows in the Chapel of the Good Shepherd were designed to enhance the architecture and serve as a teaching tool. The faceted glass clerestory windows tell the stories of the Old and New Testaments. *Opposite page, left,* The tall narthex windows progress from Biblical and historical saints on top to modern Anglican saints and finally, at eye level, to "everyday saints"—students engaged in school activities. The progression reminds children that their daily activities glorify God. *Opposite page, right,* The Great Commission window over the entrance is a call to action.

Much thought and careful planning went into the chapel design, which would have a 450-seat capacity, or enough to seat one School division. Architects **Scott Simmons** and **Ron Geyer** of Craig Gaulden Davis considered the opinions of students, faculty, parents, and alumni before deciding on a traditional English Parliament layout where members faced one another across an aisle. This configuration would better connect students and faculty during services.

The question of where to locate the chapel evoked an impassioned discussion. Initially, it was to go in the space between the new Lower School and the McCall Field House. But in the end, the Chapel of the Good Shepherd was built at the "heart" of campus. This location was chosen not only for convenient access by each division, but also as an acknowledgement of the importance of faith to a CCES education. Unfortunately, this site conflicted with an amphitheater named in memory of **Blair Babb Smoak '93**, who died in 1992. The Smoak family graciously agreed to relocate the memorial to a garden outside the Upper School, and a board member commissioned a bronze sculpture of Blair to overlook the garden.

Alumnus **Samuel (Sam) W. Smith III '82** supervised the chapel construction through his firm, Triangle Construction, which had also managed the renovation of the former Upper School and the construction of the Middle School in 1994. Smith's even temperament and vested interest in the project were invaluable in handling a myriad of details, from lighting to stained glass windows.

Crosby Willet of Willet-Hauser Studios in Philadelphia created the magnificent chapel windows. They used stained glass for the massive window above the entrance depicting the Great Commission, for the beautiful abstract design above the altar representing the Eucharistic bread and wine, and for the narthex windows. Faceted glass was chosen for the clerestory windows illustrating Old and New Testament stories. Long, narrow windows in the narthex celebrate Saints Mark, Luke, Paul, and Stephen as well as students at the School, who are reading, playing instruments, and engaging in sports.

"The Chapel is designed to teach through imagery and symbolism," Simmons told an audience during the dedication service on September 8, 2005. "Like the ancient cathedrals built in a pre-literate age, many of us have become illiterate of the teachings found in scripture and of our own Christian heritage. The Chapel is here to reclaim that heritage and to offer a quiet place of reflection and teaching in the midst of a busy campus," he said. Today the chapel is a "sacred space" on campus—a place of worship and peace for all who enter.

FUTURE GROWTH

When construction finally ended and the last vestiges of equipment and building supplies disappeared, a general sense of pride pervaded the School. No longer was CCES

The entire school lined the Blair Babb Smoak Amphitheater for the chapel groundbreaking in 2004.

Board Chair Frances Ellison and Charles Mickel with preliminary plans for the chapel. As Chair of the Chapel Committee, Mickel was a driving force behind the building of the chapel.

Rector Bob Dannals preaches at the dedication of the Chapel of the Good Shepherd on May 8, 2005. Bishop Dorsey F. Henderson, Jr., *seated*, celebrated the joyous service.

The Chapel of the Good Shepherd seen through the berry-laden branches of a dogwood tree.

split between two locations, and a chapel sat prominently in the midst of three attractive, updated academic buildings. With the addition of the Cavalier Training Center in 2006, there were also updated facilities for the growing athletic program.

Even so, the desire to improve the campus is ongoing. Today there are discussions about creating an additional gymnasium, areas for instrumental music and the other fine arts, an achievement center for tutoring and enrichment, and resurfacing the track and the tennis courts. The vision of our leaders and the generosity of our community will undoubtly continue to be the driving forces for these changes. In the meantime, students can take pride in their very special place to grow.

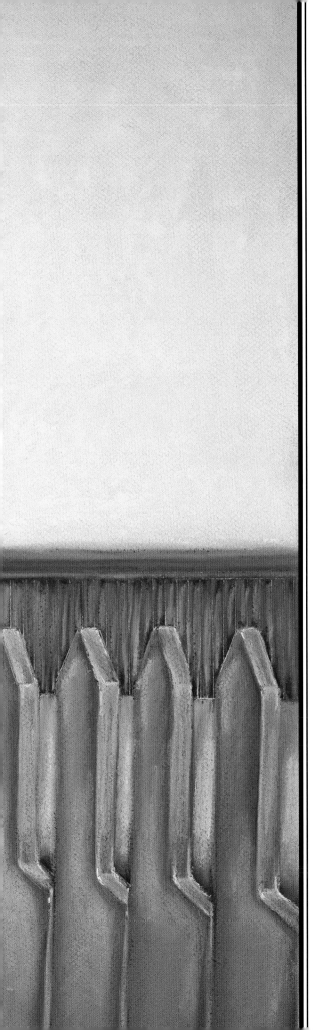

A CHRISTIAN EDUCATION AND A CARING COMMUNITY

The High Road

Building this School has been a pilgrimage of sorts, a spiritual journey intended to shape the character of students as much as their minds. Christ Church Episcopal School has never forgotten its origin as a church school, and when it became necessary to separate the Church and the School, CCES built a magnificent chapel at the heart of campus to symbolize the central role of Christian faith and worship to the school community.

CHAPTER

4

Father Chuck Blanck with a group of students outside Markley Chapel in the 60s when girls wore chapel caps at services.

Father Roberts believed that a school offering academic excellence in a Christian setting was vital to Greenville. He was certain that such an institution would positively influence the community, and that it was worthy of the Church's time and resources. He saw a chance to shape not only the minds of the rising generations but also their hearts. If the graduates of CCES possessed both academic acumen as well as a natural propensity toward stewardship, they would be leaders and contributors wherever they went.

In defense of opening a Christian school, Guthrie, the School's first Headmaster, told *The Greenville News* in 1959, "Christianity involves living, and therefore Christian education involves the intellectual and social life….All Christian education taught in the School will be as the Episcopal Church holds it."

At first Christian Education (CE) classes were assigned to church volunteers, such as Genevieve Shirley and Page Scovil. But with the addition of ninth grade in 1961, the responsibility became more than these women could manage alone. Father Carson agreed to teach the seniors an in-depth religion class, and later he assigned classes to **The Reverend Chuck Blanck**, an Associate Rector with a gift for working with young students.

When Canon Bray became Headmaster, he established CE requirements for graduation, including one term in ninth grade and two terms in grades 10–12. Again, Carson chose a member of the Christ Church clergy to teach these classes.

Today all students from Primer through grade 8 take CE for at least one term during the year. In the Upper School, in order to graduate, all students must complete three semesters of religious studies, including Old Testament, New Testament, and Ethics and Spirituality. In addition, they must complete fifteen hours of service learning each year for a total of sixty hours.

PRAYER AND WORSHIP

Prayer is woven into the life of the School, not only in chapel, but also in the classroom and on the athletic field. Headmaster Bethea once said, "An Episcopal school is one in which the people are not ashamed to seek the help of God." He said there was a fundamentally different approach to life and learning between Episcopal schools and secular schools. He also said there were differences between a "church school and one with the word 'Episcopal' in its title."

The church-school teacher should know something about sin — including his own; something about the nature of forgiveness. Our teachers should know something about "The General Confession" and say it in the company of our students. Our teachers should certainly work to create a community of those who teach and those who learn in which there can be real intercessory between human beings, not simply a handing out of information from the "voice of authority."

The School's first graduating seniors, the Class of 1972.

In 1959 students gathered in the chapel daily, attending worship services three times a week. Today students attend one Eucharistic and one prayer service each week. Services follow the Episcopal liturgy but are adapted to the students' level. Beginning in fourth grade, students serve as acolytes and give readings at the lectern, while in the Upper School students acolyte in turn with their advisee groups. They lend their musical talents to services and receive such honors as the Fine Arts and Epiphany Scholar awards during special services. Thus, student achievement is placed within the context of using one's talents to glorify God.

Traditional ceremonies such as Commencement and Awards Night take place at Christ Church. Dating back to 1972, girls in long white dresses and boys in navy blazers conclude their CCES education with a church ceremony that is not only a service of thanksgiving but also an acknowledgement of God's presence in all achievements.

From 1971–2004, chapel services on the Cavalier Campus were held in the auditorium using a portable altar.

Students may serve as acolytes beginning in the fourth grade. Here, they light candles at Christ Church downtown.

Bishop Henderson seems amused by students' excitement during dedication of the new Lower School in 2002.

Members of the Honor Council watch as a student signs the Honor Code in 2004. All Middle and Upper School students sign the code during special chapel services held at the beginning of each school year.

MORAL EDUCATION

From the beginning, teachers were expected to be role models. Students responded by taking initiatives of their own toward maintaining a morally strong school. In 1970 **Michael Blakely '70**, **Caleb Freeman '72**, **Glyn Sandzen '73**, **Amy Sutherland '72**, and **Mimi Wyche '70** formed a committee to create an honor system. Four months later, the student body approved it by a vote of 80 percent, and grades 7–12 began pledging "not to lie, cheat, steal or tolerate those who do."

Now the Upper School Honor Council, consisting of students in grades 9–12, along with faculty representatives and the Senior Chaplain, considers all breaches of the Honor Code. The students present their findings and then recommend a punishment. There is tremendous respect for the Council and the Honor Code since it supports and protects an unusually trusting environment.

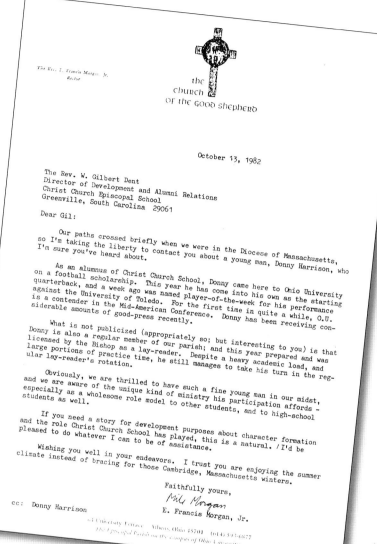

the church
of the good shepherd

The Rev. E. Francis Morgan, Jr.
Rector

October 13, 1982

The Rev. W. Gilbert Dent
Director of Development and Alumni Relations
Christ Church Episcopal School
Greenville, South Carolina 29061

Dear Gil:

Our paths crossed briefly when we were in the Diocese of Massachusetts, so I'm taking the liberty to contact you about a young man, Donny Harrison, who I'm sure you've heard about.

As an alumnus of Christ Church School, Donny came here to Ohio University on a football scholarship. This year he has come into his own as the starting quarterback, and a week ago was named player-of-the-week for his performance against the University of Toledo. For the first time in quite a while, O.U. is a contender in the Mid-American Conference. Donny has been receiving considerable amounts of good-press recently.

What is not publicized (appropriately so; but interesting to you) is that Donny is also a regular member of our parish; and this year prepared and was licensed by the Bishop as a lay-reader. Despite a heavy academic load, and large portions of practice time, he still manages to take his turn in the regular lay-reader's rotation.

Obviously, we are thrilled to have such a fine young man in our midst, and we are aware of the unique kind of ministry his participation affords - especially as a wholesome role model to other students, and to high-school students as well.

If you need a story for development purposes about character formation and the role Christ Church School has played, this is a natural. I'd be pleased to do whatever I can to be of assistance.

Wishing you well in your endeavors. I trust you are enjoying the summer climate instead of bracing for those Cambridge, Massachusetts winters.

Faithfully yours,

Phil Morgan

E. Francis Morgan, Jr.

cc: Donny Harrison

A CCES education nurtures mind, body, and soul equally, as evident in this tribute to Donny Harrison '79 from the rector of a church near Ohio University where Donny attended on a football scholarship.

A CARING COMMUNITY

CCES has always emphasized the importance of caring for others. In an orientation speech to his faculty in 1972, Bethea called on the faculty to "love" the students because he knew they would in turn reflect this love outward.

> *I get back to an awfully overworked word in our language. I know that you, like me, wish we could get some people to use it less. This word is LOVE. But when we're looking at these [children] and listening to them, we can't be doing any less than really loving them. Not sentimental love – but something a lot deeper.*

> *I put it to you right here: You have been called to the task you're facing: the task of teaching; to the task of running this School and this Church. And I can only urge each of you to do everything possible to love each and every one of [our students].*

Special Friends Day in the Lower School and Grandparents Day in the Middle and Upper Schools foster a sense of community among students, families, and friends. Here, John Flanagan '10 and Tony Klutz '01 as "special friends" at the downtown campus.

A receptive audience took the Headmaster's words to heart. The faculty fostered an atmosphere in which high academic expectations were accompanied by constant encouragement. They looked to one another to maintain a tone of kindness in the classroom, in the hallways, and on the fields. Naturally, students excelled in this environment, growing in confidence and understanding of their worth.

Jean Cochran remembered teaching a student whose mother had recently been buried in the churchyard. Instinctively, she would take the young boy's hand when they passed the grave, sensing the pain he was quietly enduring. Neither teacher nor child spoke of the gesture for it was simply a natural extension of their classroom relationship.

Throughout the School's history, there have been many who have faced tragedy. But each time, a certain teacher or staff member penetrated the dark days with encouragement enough to see the child through.

My personal challenge came when I was just fifteen, in 1976, in the ninth grade when my father suddenly died of a massive heart attack. It was then that I believe I began to realize and appreciate how special CCES truly was. Following my father's death, CCES staff members visited our home, attended the funeral, and offered incredible support during the following rough times. One day, Mrs. Mary Roper stopped me in the hallway and sat down with me on a bench beside the wall. She told me that she had known my father well and had traded with him at his pharmacy for many years. She said many very nice things about him, offered her sympathies to me and encouraged me to be strong and continue in school. She was warmly sincere and in her usual manner, firm. It was several months later that I learned that Mrs. Roper had cancer, and she died the following year.

—**Jan W. Shaw '79**

In 1991 Christ Church established the Epiphany Scholarship "to honor a student who exemplifies commitment to Christian values through worship, sensitivity and outreach to others, personal manifestation of love of God and God's people." In 1999 Jenny Pressly '99 was awarded the scholarship. *From left to right,* Senior Chaplain John Pollock, Head of School Ellen Moceri, Anna Pressley '62 (Jenny's mother), Jenny, former English teacher Florence Pressly (her grandmother), Rector Bob Dannals, and Middle School Chaplain Joe Britt.

SERVICE LEARNING

In the 60s, 70s, and 80s, community service was voluntary and most likely to occur at Thanksgiving and Christmas. Headmaster Bethea would suggest in his newsletter that children bring canned goods for the Church Home at York or a local charity. Later in the mid-70s when there were two campuses, the Upper School advisee groups often adopted a needy family for the holiday season.

I had Mary Roper for ninth-grade science. I enjoyed her class and her "one, two, I said TWO ..." But what I really remember was [that] she was the teacher who helped our class with our Christmas family. Our grade adopted a family, complete with tree decorations, gifts, clothes, food and delivery. We had so much stuff that we ended up taking on about six or seven families. Her science lab turned into a distribution/gift wrap center. Delivering the things was a very eye-opening experience for most of us. No matter how hard I try or how much I give, I have never been able to recapture the good feeling I had that Christmas.

—Gage Hipp Caulder '77

There were also opportunities to serve the School itself beginning in the early 60s. Students could become involved in school government, participate in chapel services, or help maintain the campus. One 1982 report noted that "100% of students participated in one or more of the following school assistance programs: Beautification of grounds; Indoor cleaning assistance; Upper School tutorial assistance for Middle School; Honor Council; Student Government; Lunch Room clean-up; Altar Guild; Acolytes, Chapel ushers and readers; and Special Fundraising Projects for school activities."

In 1989 the idea of adding more structure to service efforts gained appeal. Minor M. Shaw, Jim Pressly, **Gary Thompson**, and Lower School Director Becky Brown organized a program specifically for sophomores to help them "understand the concepts of community responsibility and leadership." Upper School English teacher **Betty Cavan** (1978–2001) became the faculty coordinator along with Brown, and together they developed a curriculum to educate tenth-graders about the realities of poverty.

Headmaster Rumrill enthusiastically endorsed the new class, suggesting a format similar to the "Leadership Greenville" program of the Chamber of Commerce. Students would visit agencies for the poor and then return to role-play scenarios that might have led to severe financial hardship. The program gained additional momentum in 1992 when Rumrill hired the School's first Student Body President, **Anna Dunson Pressly '62**, to be Director of Community Service.

She built upon the efforts of Cavan and Brown by setting up weekly volunteer engagements for Middle and Upper School students. Pressly and Cavan organized an after-school program

First-grader Julia Jay '77 and Primer Howard Newton '78 admire the presents on display in Markley Chapel in 1965. Teaching students to care for the needy has been part of the school philosophy since the beginning.

When Anna Pressly '62 became the School's first community service coordinator in 1993, she involved students in a variety of projects, such as this Habitat for Humanity renovation on Doe Street, *below*. In later years Upper School students have helped build Habitat houses in Greenville, and Middle School students, *left*, too young to be allowed on a construction site, have worked on school property to put together door and window frames for Habitat houses.

Below, third-grader Bailey Byrum '13 playing bingo with an Alzheimer's patient at Greenville Place. In the Lower School students are introduced to age-appropriate community service activities.

Today, students as young as first-graders visit the needy through the School's Service Learning program. *Below*, Hunter Kuykendall '13, Haigen Mirando '13, and Asheton Hinton '13 at a Meals-on-Wheels delivery in 2005.

Campus and community beautification projects are perennial service activities. Here, during Senior Week, students paint a fence in Greenville's Cleveland Park.

in the gymnasium where sophomores and fifth-graders mentored children at Camp Opportunity. Pressly never knew "who gained more from the experience: those who were giving help or those who were receiving attention."

Jean Forte Carter (1996–2005) became Community Service Director on a part-time basis from 1999–2005. She advised the Volunteer Club, which looked for groups that needed assistance. Many students who participated were shaped by their experiences. One of them, **Melissa Morrow '00**, became a summer counselor at Camp Opportunity after working with the organization through school. Later, while studying architecture at Clemson, Morrow designed a facility for the camp.

Had I not attended Christ Church Episcopal School for 13 years, I would not be where I am today. I would not have begun working with the children of Camp Opportunity in the eighth grade. I would not have stayed involved with the organization after graduation.

—Melissa Morrow

In 2005 after teaching second grade in the Lower School for six years, **Elizabeth Sterling Jarrett '82** (1999–present) became the full-time Director of Service Learning, a title meant to convey the expectation that service would become a learned and lasting part of each student's behavior. "It was where my heart was," Jarrett said. "Our children have so many opportunities here, and I wanted to help them learn to serve the needs of others who haven't been so blessed."

Beginning in 2007 the Service Learning program has sponsored a ten-day summer mission trip to Ecuador for students and faculty. Students become involved in manual labor, teaching, and other service projects.

At a picnic sponsored by the English for Speakers of Other Languages (ESOL) program, a young student enjoys that most American of picnic treats: s'mores.

Today Jarrett organizes service opportunities for all three School divisions, progressing from simple gestures in the lower grades, such as playing with the preschoolers at A Child's Haven, to larger projects, such as disaster relief, in the upper grades. To fulfill their fifteen hours of service learning each year, Upper School students may participate in the Volunteer Club or initiate their own service projects. The goal is for CCES graduates to "leave with hearts and minds open to the community." The fact that many students launch their own service programs for their Sophomore Project and the Senior Thesis suggests that students take seriously the expectation of giving back to the community. During the 2008–09 school year, Jarrett estimated that CCES students completed almost 8,000 hours of community service.

RESPECT FOR DIVERSITY

Bethea and his predecessor, Guthrie, upheld the principle that Episcopal schools would not discriminate against people of other faiths or backgrounds. In 1966 Bethea hired **Clanton G. Anchors, Jr.** (1966–68), a brilliant math teacher who was both blind and crippled but had the ability to conduct an orderly class. Bethea also enrolled the first African American children in 1968, and in 1972 he welcomed the first foreign exchange student, **Daniela Dacco** of Cremona, Italy, through the American Field Service (AFS) program.

The Heads who followed Bethea also embraced this belief. They understood the benefits of openness toward all people and the hypocrisy of a Christian institution that would turn its back on anyone with differences. Bray, for whom the Canon Bray Memorial Scholarship for Students of Color is named, made a point to reach out to everyone in the student body equally. In this way, he shaped precedent.

As juniors, IB diploma students participate in a group service project. Here, Rick Furman '07 serves in the Lapsits for Literacy program with the one-year-olds at the Golden Rule Child Development Center in Simpsonville.

The message was not lost on students. In a letter to Cathy Jones (1966–95), **Laurie Steinman Watral '77** wrote:

The first thing that stands out in my mind about my years at CCES was the fact that I was one of two Jewish kids in a private, Episcopal school. That alone is a major event in and of itself! I remember addressing the student body – I think it was my senior year – about the Jewish holidays that occur in September. Canon Bray approached me and hoped that I would share my cultural and religious celebrations with the school. Not only was I terrified to speak publicly, but I was horrified to validate my cultural differences. Somehow I did it. I remember how you responded to me after my speech with tears of pride in your eyes. I knew then what I had done was worth it.

In 1988 CCES became a member of the National Association of Episcopal Schools (NAES), a group that embraces certain principles common to all Episcopal schools. Among these is the belief that "Episcopal Schools are created to be communities that honor, celebrate and worship God as the center of life. They are created to serve God in Christ in all persons, regardless of origin, background, ability or religion."

Today, the student body includes a broad cross-section of nationalities and cultures, reflecting, in part, growing diversity within the Greenville population. Since 2006 a part-time Director of Diversity, **Greg Hood**, has worked with the Admission Office to attract qualified candidates for whom a CCES education will

The teaching of values is woven into the life of the School in so many ways. Here, a class performs a song at Fourth Grade Recognition in Markley Chapel.

make an important difference in their lives, and whose backgrounds and experiences will enhance the breadth of the student body.

THE SEPARATION OF CHURCH AND SCHOOL

During and after the separation of Church and School in 2001, concerns arose over the identity of an Episcopal school physically and financially separate from its Church. Rector Dannals arrested the uncertainty. He said the very name, Christ Church Episcopal School, obligated CCES to remain under "the appropriate and applicable canons of the Episcopal Church and the authority of the Bishop." He emphasized, "We are still an Episcopal school in every way."

The role of the School Chaplain was most affected by the separation. In 2004 Dr. Cox hired The Reverend Richard Grimball to serve the School exclusively. Instead of splitting time between the Church and the School as earlier chaplains had done, Grimball was hired to minister primarily to the School community, now a congregation within itself. He came to oversee the Christian Education program, conduct weekly worship services, and manage a team of lay chaplains. Today Grimball, Middle School Chaplain Joe Britt (1986–present), and Lower School Chaplain Valerie Morris Riddle (1997–present) minister to families, students, and employees.

Many things distinguish CCES from other schools but none more than its Episcopal tradition, its emphasis on the moral and character development of students, and its caring community. It is a place where administrators and teachers nurture students through compassion and love and thereby shape minds as well as hearts.

Valerie (Morris) Riddle, known as "Miss Valerie" in the Lower School, is beloved as a chaplain. Through her gentle personality and ability to engage students body and soul in a variety of activities, she has done much to transform Christian education, worship, and service programs in the Lower School.

At the last outdoor chapel held downtown in May 2002, acolytes file down the steps of the Parish House with Miss Valerie.

The Guidebook

While mapping a journey, a traveler may consult a few guidebooks. A student embarking on a CCES education will have, as a primary guidebook, the School's curriculum. The rigorous academic content and standards at CCES become the student's detailed itinerary, leading him from childhood to college and a lifetime of service, leadership, and civic responsibility. The itineraries have changed with the times, but the destination has not. The destination is, and always has been, an exceptional education.

CHAPTER

5

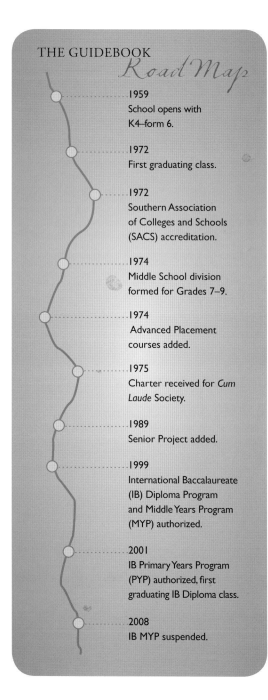

THE GUIDEBOOK
Road Map

1959
School opens with
K4–form 6.

1972
First graduating class.

1972
Southern Association
of Colleges and Schools
(SACS) accreditation.

1974
Middle School division
formed for Grades 7–9.

1974
Advanced Placement
courses added.

1975
Charter received for *Cum
Laude* Society.

1989
Senior Project added.

1999
International Baccalaureate
(IB) Diploma Program
and Middle Years Program
(MYP) authorized.

2001
IB Primary Years Program
(PYP) authorized, first
graduating IB Diploma class.

2008
IB MYP suspended.

CURRICULUM

While many changes have taken place at CCES since 1959, the basic purposes and methods agreed upon by the founders have continued to guide the ongoing pursuit of academic excellence. Since its inception, the School's strong curriculum has been built on a solid classical foundation, but it has also proven to be flexible enough to address social and technological advances.

In 1961 Christ Church Vestry member Gaston Jennings wrote the following response to a question about the goals of education at CCES:

> *For what are we attempting to educate our children? The School recognizes the need for flexible teaching and subject matter as we are educating these children for a world about which we know nothing. No one knows what this world will be in 5, 10 or 15 years. Our purpose therefore might be summed up by saying that the results the school is attempting to achieve are that each child receive an education that will permit him to live a God-centered life using the talents and abilities which God has given him to the greatest degree possible in this life.*

This philosophy has guided curriculum decisions throughout the decades. Each school head has sought to preserve a traditional approach to learning while also incorporating sound new pedagogy.

In 1974 Allen Bray arrived with the goal of making CCES academically more rigorous. Up to this point, all grades had followed a standard classical curriculum. Within months, he increased the graduation requirements to four units of English; three units of history, mathematics, and science; and two units of classical or foreign language. He also required two units of physical education and two units of elective studies. It was to prevent "an eleventh-grade peaking," he said.

At nearly the same time, Bray began to offer Advanced Placement (AP) courses, beginning with AP Latin in 1974. These classes exposed exceptionally motivated students to college-level courses. Additionally, they gave the School further distinction in terms of its curriculum among colleges and universities.

During Bray's tenure the Foreign Language Department expanded under the direction of **Edward (Mr. O) Olechovsky** (1973–80). In 1975 seventh-grade students began learning a classical language, choosing from French, Latin, or Spanish

All sophomore students present a Personal Project on a subject of their choosing to classmates and family members. Similar to the Senior Thesis, the months-long project is mentored by a faculty member and allows students to launch community service projects, learn new skills, or research topics of interest.

"in order to obtain a strong, solid facility by the senior year," Olechovsky said. With this change came the need for more faculty who could teach advanced-level French and Spanish classes, like those Georgia Frothingham (1965–91) and **Lynn McColl** (1973–97) were already offering in Latin. Among the new instructors was Panamanian-born **Chris (Fred) Hearon** (1975–97, 2003–08), who became the Language Department Chair in 1978. Hearon endorsed a more sequential approach to learning foreign language as opposed to mastering separate blocks of material. His philosophy fit well with Bray's new requirements in which students needed at least two full years of foreign language to graduate. Furthermore, it coincided with an increase in international students that began in the late 80s and 90s.

In 1999 under Ellen Moceri's leadership the School received authorization for the International Baccalaureate (IB) Diploma Program for grades 11–12, and the Middle Years Program (MYP) for grades 6–10. In 2001 the Lower School

Georgia (Doc) Frothingham
(1965–91)

Soon after becoming Rector in 1964, Father Carson hired Georgia Frothingham, sensing from his first meeting he had found a "remarkable person." Years later, in 2001, Carson delivered a homily filled with admiration for the life of this beloved teacher.

"Doc," as she was known to many of her students, was a very special person. [She was a] teacher, tutor, confidant and friend to countless children -- two of ours. I can still hear her walking down the hall saying, "But Father Carson, Latin is essential to any person who wants to be known as an educated person. …"

In her life and ministry, there is a message for you and me: faith and the practice of religion were not options for her, but rather essential for the formation of a whole and total human being. It was her style, and if one didn't get that from her, the person missed the most important message she had to communicate.

— Tom Carson

Dr. Georgia Frothingham's name was synonymous with Latin for the twenty-seven years she shaped students' minds at CCES.

In 1990 the CCES Alumni Association announced an endowment in her name to provide financial aid for children of alumni. In 1992 and every year since, the Alumni Golf Tournament has raised funds for the Georgia Frothingham Scholarship Endowment.

was authorized for the Primary Years Program (PYP) in grades Primer– 5. At that point CCES had the distinction of being one of a handful of independent schools in North America to offer the full continuum of IB programs.

Originating in the mid-70s, the IB program was an attempt to establish consistently high academic standards on an international basis so that any student with an IB diploma from any country in the world would be measured against the same rigorous criteria. Inquiry learning and reflection are central to the IB curricular framework, enabling students to become lifelong learners and critical thinkers.

By aligning with an increasingly global world, the IB curriculum gained favor among many American universities. It seemed a natural fit for a college preparatory school like CCES, especially as the student body expanded to include more international students. It also seemed to complement the School's existing standards and philosophy. In the Upper School, juniors and seniors now had the option to pursue Advanced Placement or IB courses or both; those students who followed the rigorous IB requirements in grades 11–12 could earn the IB diploma.

Today's technology courses could be said to have originated in Nancy Baker's typing classes.

Faye Jay uses an overhead projector to teach math in the mid-70s. Today classrooms are equipped with SMART Boards, digital projectors, and surround sound technology.

SMART Boards are not merely high-tech versions of the whiteboard; with web connectivity they are teaching resources that bring the world directly into the classroom.

In the Lower and Middle Schools the IB Primary Years Program (PYP) and Middle Years Program (MYP) provided a framework for the existing curricula, and many teachers found the new approach energizing. With training, the CCES faculty embraced the IB philosophy, and several teachers gained national recognition as international IB trainers, site visitors, and workshop leaders.

CCES continues to assess the value of the IB program in the same way it regularly re-examines its entire curriculum. In 2008 the administration decided to drop the MYP in grades 5–10, keeping only the sophomore Personal Project.

This project, as well as the required Senior Thesis or IB Extended Essay in twelfth grade, exemplifies the academic process at CCES. Students choose topics and activities of personal interest, and for several months they receive individual attention from a faculty mentor who guides them through each stage of work. Some students delve into an academic topic, while others design and execute their own community projects. Still others pursue a hobby or a career possibility. Through the required oral presentation students gain self-confidence, poise, and ease in public speaking. Ultimately, these "capstone experiences" figure significantly in the process of helping each student realize his or her individual potential. For some, these projects become interests they will pursue throughout their lives.

Graduates of the International Baccalaureate Diploma Program wear an IB medal cast specially for CCES. Here, one 2003 graduate helps another adjust her medal before Commencement.

Over the years there have been many exceptional projects. "Mice on Main" by **Jimmy Ryan '00** remains one of the School's most memorable. Ryan's nine bronze mice, which he placed strategically throughout Main Street, preceded the proliferation of sculptures downtown. Today they continue to give joy to children who find them. In 2008 the city of Greenville publicized the mice in a tourism brochure, on its website, and on tee shirts.

Similarly, **Ingram Carpenter**'s Senior Thesis in 2006 made a difference in the Greenville community. For several years CCES students had been volunteering with the John Wesley United Methodist Church Breakfast Kitchen through the School's Service Learning program. When DHEC regulations closed the kitchen, Carpenter raised more than $100,000 to pay for renovations. Now the "Susan Ingram Carpenter Breakfast Kitchen" continues to serve hot breakfast to the homeless and the needy.

The strength of the School's college-preparatory curriculum is evidenced by the fact that 100 percent of CCES graduates are accepted into colleges of their choice. SAT scores are 300–400 points higher than the average national and South Carolina scores, and as of 2009, CCES has produced 147 National Merit Finalists. CCES offers approximately twenty AP classes. The students who take these intensive classes, sometimes as early as grade 10, must take a College Board examination and receive a score of at least three out of a possible five to earn college credit. And while these statistics are certainly one measure of success, an equally important measure is the number of academically average students who have risen above expectations because of teachers who believed in them.

A FACULTY OF CONSISTENTLY HIGH CALIBER

When Tom Roberts and Claude Guthrie were establishing goals in 1959, they decided that a remarkable faculty was essential to an excellent education. They carefully chose individuals who would uphold their commitment to superior teaching, drawing on parishioners and the former St. James School faculty.

"We had the reputation of having the cream of the crop of public school teachers in the county," Guthrie said in a 1985 interview. "If a teacher in the county felt that she was good, it was an embarrassment not to be teaching at CCES."

"[Most of] the teachers were selected from the Parish back then," said English Department Chair Florence Pressly, referring to the early years when the Rector had final authority over hiring. "Rufus Bethea approached each one of us individually. We had a commitment beyond being just a teacher. It was a feeling that we were doing something for our Church because the School was our main mission. We tried to be friends with the children while still maintaining the teacher/student relationship."

Students have always understood, perhaps even more so with the passage of time, that CCES teachers were demanding and highly attentive out of love and concern. Invariably, they responded to such attention with a desire to meet

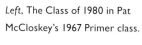

Left, The Class of 1980 in Pat McCloskey's 1967 Primer class.

Below, For more than thirty years Lower School Teacher Assistant Josie Burdine has earned the affection of students in the Primer classes. Many a senior returns to her for a hug before graduation.

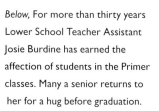

Left, English teacher Betty Cavan focuses intently on a student. Small class sizes enable teachers to give students individual attention and help them reach their potential.

expectations. **Nancy Neff Madeoy '76** recalled:

> *The teacher that influenced me most during my CCES years was **Mr. [Mike] Stafford**, the math teacher in the Upper School.... One reason I remember him best was that he always encouraged me to do my best even when I felt discouraged. He didn't allow me to give up.*

Over the course of fifty years, countless instructors have distinguished themselves as being exceptional in their fields, but proper acknowledgement of them all is not possible within the confines of a brief history. Their length of service, their uncompromising standards, their connection to students, and the impact of their instruction should never be forgotten or underestimated. (See page 140 for faculty with more than five years of service.)

Committed as ever, today's faculty has grown from 17 in 1959 to more than 110 in 2009. Three out of four teachers hold master's degrees, and a few, particularly in the Upper School, have doctoral degrees.

Often, CCES teachers form deep friendships during their years together. Jim Rumrill felt this unusual closeness among his faculty was an attribute worth acknowledging. He knew **Pat McCloskey** (1964–74) and **Faye Jay** (1963–87) had long been hosting luncheons for former teachers to reminisce about their school days. In 1996 he gave the Golden Cavaliers, as they had begun to call themselves, recognition as an official School organization chartered by the board.

Now this distinguished group meets monthly at the Poinsett Club for lunch. They also come to campus each year for a chapel service and luncheon so they can learn of recent developments and significant changes.

Florence Pressly
(1968–74)

In addition to being, with her husband Jim, among the first benefactors of the School, Florence Pressly began teaching English in 1968. She was one of a core group of teachers who maintained a successful academic environment in spite of the unorthodox surroundings at the YMCA and Textile Hall. In 1971 she and Cathy Jones organized the first of two student trips abroad to supplement classroom instruction. Nearly forty years later, many graduates still talk about the impressionable year they spent at "Christ High at the Y" and the summers they traveled with Mrs. Pressly.

To this day many of Florence Pressly's former students keep in contact with her.

I remember being impressed with Mrs. Florence Pressly, Mrs. Cathy Jones, Mrs. Barbara Harrison, and a host of others because they did not have to teach. They had successful husbands and could have stayed home or worked in other fields. But our teachers taught because they loved to teach, and we loved them in return. They were our advisors and our friends.

—John Scovil '73

In 1972 Florence Pressly and Cathy Jones took students on a magical thirty-eight-day tour of England, Holland, Germany, Austria, Italy, Switzerland, and France. The summer before they had taken students to Greece.

Dubbed "the Poor Man's Indiana Jones," biology teacher Reggie Titmas, whose freshman "bug project" became a CCES rite of passage, in a photo from the 1983 *Hellenia*.

Dan Sellers's Class of 1975 ninth-grade trip to Washington, D.C. Dating back to Headmaster Bethea, class trips have long been an important part of the curriculum.

Headmaster Bray introduced the *Cum Laude Society* in the mid-70s to recognize juniors, seniors, and faculty who not only excelled academically but also demonstrated impeccable character. In 1981 the Society included *(seated, left to right)*, Ruth King, Jackie Gaddy (née Suber), Monte Ball, Mary Dellinger, Ginny Tate, and *(standing, left to right)*, Elizabeth Jervey '81, Maylon Hanold '81, Brian King '81, Larry Steinmeyer, Eugenia Howard, Allen Bray, Lynn McColl, Diana Stafford, Mike Stafford, and Ben Crabtree.

Headmaster Ben Crabtree surrounded by faculty members, *from left*, Barbara Carter, Cathy Jones, and Jackie Messer Rogers at the 1985 senior prom.

Ginny Tate
(1969–PRESENT)

Ginny Tate arrived in 1969 after earning a master's degree from Harvard. Looking nearly as young as the sixth and seventh-grade students she first taught, she became one of the School's most dedicated teachers. She possessed a brilliant mathematical mind and a gift for teaching. Over the years, Tate has taught several generations of CCES students, giving many alumni the gift of continuity as their own children reached Middle School.

My fourth-grade teacher was Mrs. Ginny Tate. With her guidance, I developed a love for math that took me down the path of chemical engineering at Georgia Tech. I still remember Mrs. Tate showing up for my graduation. A special lady.
—Barry Cox '77

Ginny Tate's many students have included several whose children eventually passed through her classroom too. Shown here in a photo from the 1970 *Hellenian*, she has taught at CCES for forty of its first fifty years.

Left, Pig heart dissection is a seventh-grade rite of passage, thanks to Helen Schwiers '76, who taught seventh-grade science from 1985–2006. It proved more complicated than the earlier chicken wing dissection—both for students and teacher. (One year she defrosted the frozen hearts at home, and her cats ate two of them.)

Above, With the introduction of the IB curriculum, assessment took various forms. In 2001 first-graders concluded their inquiry into weather with a performance of "Chicken Little: The Sky is Falling," a play they wrote to showcase what they had learned.

Left, Strings, guitar, drum, piano, and Middle School band programs all began to expand once the Lower School moved onto the Cavalier Campus.

They cherish being together, especially in the place where they spent so much of their lives.

INDIVIDUAL ATTENTION

In 1959 Tom Roberts wrote the first school business plan to include no more than twenty students per class "in order that each student receive the necessary amount of time from the teacher to do his best work." He knew the overcrowded public schools were short-changing many children. If he could limit class size, he believed that overall learning would accelerate, especially among intelligent students. To this end, he also required an entrance test. Guthrie explained "that the school will aim for the average and above-average student," with the intention of accepting only those students who could "profit the most from this type of school."

Former Upper School Director Bill Sparrgrove once said, "There is no place for a student to hide in our classrooms." Small classes are critical to the academic environment at CCES. The dividends that students reap from this personal attention are many. Teachers know their students' strengths and respond to their individual needs. Teachers can identify the areas where students have difficulties and offer both extra help and specific assignments to address them. The strong relationship between student and teacher does more than increase motivation. These relationships ultimately enable Upper School faculty members to write detailed personal

Barbara Harrison
(1971–92)

Barbara Harrison came to CCES in 1971 to teach sixth-grade reading. She quickly became a favorite among Lower School students, who found her enthusiasm for reading contagious. She could hold a class spellbound as she read *Old Yeller* or *The Best Christmas Pageant Ever.*

Barbara Harrison with then-sixth-grader Dena Stone '78.

She was the first teacher to make me understand the importance of learning and the pride that can be realized through hard work. School was a bit of an afterthought for this ten-year-old boy. During a book report project, she took the time to follow up with me during an assignment. She pushed me to really try and figure out what was going on and to express more than what the words simply stated. She wanted me to enjoy the book and read it for the experience and not just the assignment. I worked hard to understand a "real" book, and wanted to impress her. When the assignments were handed back, she asked me to present my report to the entire class. I was very proud as I told the whole class about The Old Man and the Sea. *To this day, if you look on the third shelf in my bedroom in my parent's house, you will see a slightly tattered blue construction paper folder with a blue marlin jumping off the cover. On the front is a big red A+ and a note from Mrs. Harrison telling me how proud she was. It changed my life.*
—Darrell Jervey '82

CCES has participated in numerous international exchange programs. Here, then-seventh-grader Jack Cebe '05 is surrounded by students at the Rikkyo School in Tokyo.

CCES third-graders crowded around Governor Richard Riley in the State House in 1979. Today, third-graders continue to visit Columbia as part of their South Carolina studies.

For several years beginning in the mid-90s, fourth-graders participated in Colonial Day, which included square dancing, colonial crafts and games, such essential chores as candle-making, and a meal of "colonial stew" (minus the beavers and squirrels).

The Staffords

DIANA (1974–2003) AND MIKE (1974–98)

Diana and Mike joined CCES in the early 70s to teach in the Upper School Science and Math Departments respectively. Very quickly, the Staffords earned reputations for patience and proficiency in their fields. Both would go to extended lengths to help struggling students by staying long after the bell to give extra instruction. Apart from teaching, Diana coached field hockey, sang in the school choir, and ran a photography darkroom while Mike coached soccer and was faculty advisor for the Outdoors Club. "[The Staffords] were the epitome of the ideal independent school faculty couple who contributed to every aspect of school life," Jim Rumrill once said.

Diana Stafford [was my favorite teacher] for the fact that her expectations of me were never coupled with that darker cousin, judgment; for providing a safety rope that never turned into a hangman's noose; for expecting more of me than I expected of myself; for having the nimblest of minds but never the need to prove it.

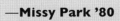
—Missy Park '80

Between them, Diana and Mike Stafford gave fifty-four years to the school—teaching, coaching, and involved in many activities outside their classrooms.

Below, Elizabeth Cleveland '98 contemplates a poison dart frog on a trip to the Costa Rican rainforest. Over the years biology teacher Reggie Titmas has offered students many opportunities to explore marine and rainforest habitats during the summer.

Right, CCES students learn to present information and be comfortable in front of an audience beginning in the earliest grades. Here, third-grade students explain holiday customs in Mexico during a performance of "Christmas Around the World" in 2000.

Right, Fifth-graders and ninth-graders enjoy outdoor experiences for bonding, team-building, and fun at the beginning of the school year. Since 1997 incoming freshmen have embarked on an overnight "mystery trip" to destinations unknown to share adventures whitewater rafting, hang-gliding, or exploring such cities as Chicago and New York. The mystery trip and the fifth-grade Paris Mountain team-building exercises also give teachers the opportunity to observe students outside an academic setting.

Renowned author Madeleine L'Engle paid a visit to CCES during the early 90s. Every year visiting authors and artists inspire students in each division.

personal college recommendations that set a student apart from other applicants.

Russell (Rip) Parks '72, a member of the first graduating class, earned a bachelor's degree and three master's degrees after high school. But, he said, it was the teachers at CCES who made the greatest impression.

Having earned a bachelor's degree and three master's degrees by age 29, I now look back on what appears to be a career in education. Do you know that I can barely remember any of the names of my college professors? The

Barbara Carter
(1971–PRESENT)

Barbara Carter began teaching seventh grade in 1971 at the downtown Lower School. In 1974 she moved to the Upper School, where she became a revered member of the English Department for her reputation of having high expectations for every person she taught. Once, a former student hung a quote above Carter's door that read, "Abandon all hope ye who enter here." It was only a jest, because Carter's uncompromising standards brought out the best in all her students.

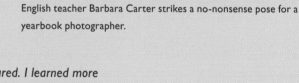

English teacher Barbara Carter strikes a no-nonsense pose for a yearbook photographer.

Mrs. Carter was my favorite teacher. She always expected the very best from us. She was firm, but I knew she cared. I learned more vocabulary [from her] in one year than I have in my lifetime. She was inspiring, and I wish my children could have the advantage of having her!!
—Elizabeth Rose McKissick '88

Jackie Suber
(1971–2005)

Jackie (Fowler Gaddy) Suber came to CCES in 1971 to teach English in the Middle and Upper Schools. It was not long before she developed a reputation for having extremely high academic expectations, tempered by a genuine interest in every student and a desire to help each one reach full potential. For Suber, teaching was a calling that did not end in the classroom. She would follow her students long after graduation. Rumrill, recognizing her unique ability to connect with people, asked her to head a new Development Office in 1989. Later, in 1995, she became Director of College Guidance for the Upper School.

Jackie Suber's genuine interest in every student and family has made her an icon at CCES.

Throughout my years in high school, teachers, classes, school buildings, and friends have changed. One thing has always stayed the same, however. That constant is Mrs. Suber's dedication to the students at our School. She has a very personal relationship with every student at our School that makes her unique.
—Patrick Dover '02

educators who had the greatest impact on my life were all at Christ Church School.

The impressions started early as I entered five-year-old kindergarten at St. James School in 1959. Then we moved into the old wooden houses along Washington Street, napping on named rugs in what surely was a former living or dining room. Soon, we were housed in what are now the Sunday school classrooms of Christ Church. There we stayed until the 9th grade. Being a member of the Class of '72, we were seniors for four years in a row. Each year, we added a grade until we eventually graduated from the newly constructed Upper School campus.

Our journey from facility to facility may have been adventurous, but it was the faculty that launched the lifelong process of learning. I distinctly remember the time I had a series of back-to-back classes that made an enormous impression on me. I had Mrs. Cathy Jones for Ancient History, Mrs. Florence Pressly for English Literature, and Dr. Georgia Frothingham for Latin. Often one class would reinforce the concepts of the other. It fit together so well. In all of my collegiate courses, I never experienced anything of equal quality.

I suppose one factor made the greatest difference between my early and later educational experiences: my teachers at CCES had a passion for what they taught, and they cared about me. Competence and caring are two halves of the same equation. Offering only one without the other robs the student of a total equation. As Abraham Kaplan, renowned 20th century philosopher and educator, wrote: "There is nothing more inspiring than having a mind unfold before you. Let people teach who have a calling. It is never just a job."

Cathy Jones
(1966–93)

Cathy Jones was a legend at CCES. She joined the faculty to teach Middle School history and stayed until her retirement in 1993. She possessed a keen wit and an unassailable understanding of American and European history. In addition, she was kind, fair, and methodical. Every ninth-grader had to learn to spell "bourgeoisie," and to learn that "World War I began because Archduke Francis Ferdinand was assassinated, NOT killed." She knew how to make the "dry, dusty and best forgotten suddenly full of mystery and an inspiration for wonder," said **Gretchen Mahon '80**.

Cathy Jones was legendary at CCES for her love of history—and of Snickers "bahs."

Catherine Jones taught me Ancient and Medieval History in the ninth grade. I will never forget her. She made learning fun and she gave me an appreciation for the past that I will be grateful for forever. She was, hands down, through all of my educational experiences (including college) the most incredible and fun teacher I ever had. Attitude is everything, hers was as positive as they come, and she passed that down to her students. I not only did well in her class. I wanted to do well.

—David Bannen '73

Side Trips and Diversions

Every journey provides opportunities for some interesting detours. Often these side trips are as memorable as the well-traveled route. The opportunities to participate in athletics, develop artistic skills, and pursue personal interests help students branch out into new areas. For some, being part of an Upper School drama production may feed a lifelong passion for engaging in community theater. For others participation on a championship soccer team may lead them one day to coach young people in the sport. Still others will forge a career from the talents they discover outside the classroom. These opportunities are not "educational frills." They are essential to forming well-rounded individuals ready to enjoy life and to enrich the lives of others.

CHAPTER

6

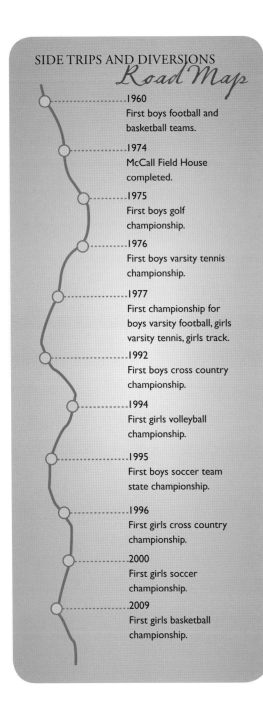

At CCES, there is the belief that the opportunities available outside the classroom are as much a part of a classical education as the academic training. Here, the School is guided by an ethos that faith in God, knowledge of one's strengths, and the ability to overcome challenges are all necessary tools to finding purpose and satisfaction in life.

For the past fifty years, CCES has devoted much time and effort to providing opportunities for students to grow and develop into well-rounded people. It has dedicated its facilities and its resources to fulfilling this mission. It has sought faculty who could bring out the artistic, athletic, and leadership talents within each student. Furthermore, it has dug deep in even the most parsimonious times to ensure that its buildings and grounds could accommodate enrichment beyond the classroom.

ATHLETICS

Before CCES was even established as an elementary school, there was talk of building an athletic program. In the summer of 1959, Arthur McCall and Sumner Williams, McCall's brother-in-law, called Rufus Bethea in Atlanta to ask if he would teach sixth grade.

It was August and they had decided to have a sixth grade, needed a teacher and wanted a man. Somehow I got the job. The boys needed something [athletically], so I worked with the fifth and sixth-grade boys after school as best I could. We had a gym and no grounds so we had to go to Cleveland Park or the YMCA. The second year we had two men who worked with sports, and the field sports were all played at the YMCA.

—Rufus Bethea

With the addition of grades 7 and 8 in 1960, there were football and basketball teams for the boys. The football schedule consisted of two opponents, Spartanburg Day School and Charlotte Country Day School. Girls participated in gym class, playing intramural basketball and volleyball on the shiny wooden floor in Finley Hall in the Parish House. There was also a cheerleading team.

By 1962 there was a formal athletic policy encouraging every student to participate. Boys began to compete in wrestling and tennis, winning the South Carolina State Tournament in tennis in the first year. There were more opponents too, including Durham Academy and Asheville Country Day School, although it meant driving longer distances for games. Additionally, girls could now compete in basketball.

CCES athletics gained momentum each year thereafter. It was clear that the opportunity to participate in team sports was an important draw to the upper grades. With this in mind, Roberts hired **Ferrell Singleton** (1962–66) to teach history and act as the first Boys Athletic Director. He also hired **J. F. Woodward** (1962–65) to be the Girls Athletic Director, a progressive move at a time when girls sports were virtually dismissed.

Singleton and Woodward added more structure and opportunity to the program. By the end of 1964, boys could compete in football, varsity and middle school basketball, wrestling, tennis, and golf. Girls had the ability to play kickball in fourth and fifth grades, Newcomb ball in sixth grade, and basketball or volleyball in ninth grade. Cheerleading continued to be popular as well.

In 1965 Bethea and Carson hired **Jim Conyers** (1965–81) as the Boys Athletic Director. His responsibilities were almost entirely to the athletic program, as opposed to those of earlier directors who also taught in the classroom. At the time of Conyers's arrival, there were no facilities to speak of beyond the Parish gymnasium with its single basketball court. Practice fields were impossible to construct because of space limitations at the Church property. Conyers therefore relied on the Cleveland Street YMCA as Bethea had done. It was not until the School expanded to the Cavalier Campus that there was finally room for practice fields.

Conyers stayed at CCES for fifteen years, instilling discipline and confidence in the many middle school boys he taught. They all responded to his quick-step walk, military haircut, and rugged colloquialisms, such as, *"I've told you this forty-eleven times!"* Many remember Conyers as the "Father of CCES Athletics," for he was instrumental in founding most of the School's teams. Today, an annual sportsmanship award in his honor goes to one boy and one girl in both the Middle and Upper Schools.

In 1968, **Millie Wilkinson**, mother of **Mary Ellen Wilkinson '74**, approached Bethea about starting a girls tennis team. When he consented, Wilkinson began holding practices at the Greenville Country Club with the help of her husband and **Judy Cromwell**, mother of **Duane '74** and **Fan '75**. Each player had previous tennis experience, but the initial success of the team was astonishing. They defeated the varsity teams at the University of Georgia, Clemson, Furman, and Radcliffe College of Harvard University in their first seasons. "We drove the girls all over to insure that they had enough competition for their abilities," Wilkinson said. They also played local secondary schools, such as Belton, J. L. Mann, Greenville High, and Spartanburg Day.

Before the Booster Club Pavilion was erected in 1999, coaches and game announcers climbed ladders to "The Tower," also known as "Partee's Perch," a rough and precarious structure slung between telephone poles that swayed when its occupants stomped and cheered.

CCES added soccer to its list of field sports in the 70s. Here, *from left,* Jimmy Parham '77 and David Weinstein '77 on the field.

Middle School PE teacher Ellen Donkle '74 poses with her JV hockey players.

From the beginning, the CCES girls tennis team was formidable. Here, members of the 1972 team pose at the Greenville Country Club where they played home matches until 1974 when the School could afford to install its own courts. *From left to right, front row,* Nancy Yeargin '73, Marty Rosson '75, Mary Ellen Wilkinson '74; *back row,* Candy McCall '73, Fannie Cromwell '75, and Libba Galloway '75.

By 1972 the tennis team was unstoppable. They had added **Nancy Yeargin Furman '73**, a state champion in her age group, who went on to play at Wimbledon. But even with this clear domination, the Cavaliers had to play without home courts until 1974.

Jim Tate joined the staff in January 1969 as a mathematics teacher and coach. Initially, he coached JV basketball and baseball and assisted Conyers with varsity football, which included boys up to eleventh grade. He became the Upper School Athletic Director when the new campus opened in 1972, deferring first to Conyers, for whom he had tremendous respect.

> *[Conyers] and I were great friends, and he was a father figure in my early years with him. He was highly respected, greatly loved and appreciated by faculty and parents alike, and he decided that as we evolved into a high school he would be most comfortable in the capacity of junior high athletic director and coach.*
>
> —Jim Tate

During the early 70s, several sports emerged as new opportunities. Among these were field hockey and boys soccer. **Anne Hassold**, a new parent with experience in northern team sports, agreed to coach the first varsity girls field hockey team in 1971. Her oldest son, **Rob '72**, brought instant distinction to the fledgling soccer team.

In 1972 **Linda Reeves** (1972–2001) joined the staff as Girls Athletic Director. Quiet and reserved, she became an inspiration for literally hundreds of CCES girls who played team sports. Reeves coached both championship and novice teams with equal interest and optimism. She also knew how to cultivate friendships with her players without compromising her authority.

Below, For almost thirty years Girls Athletic Director Linda Reeves coached novice and championship teams with equal enthusiasm. A few months before her death in 2001, she was lured back to campus for the surprise dedication of Reeves Field, where a crowd of emotional students, parents, and alumni had gathered to honor her.

I loved Linda Reeves as she would push, push and fuss on the hockey field and then just laugh and cry with all of us, encouraging us all along the way. She was so real. [I] loved Linda!

—Kendall Taylor Huguley '83

With Tate and Reeves as Athletic Directors in the Upper School, the sports program had the leadership to expand. Enthusiasm and resourcefulness compensated for primitive facilities.

Our boys dressed out in trailers (the 18-wheeler variety) that were backed up into the tree line at the scoreboard-end of the field. We had three separate trailers to accommodate our varsity, JV and junior high teams. The trailers were obviously not air-conditioned, so we had large floor fans to try and circulate air and lessen the stench that went with sweaty practice uniforms.

Our track team practiced on the football field where I had marked off a 330-yard oval with buried flag markers on the curves. Our pole vault pit was a pile of used tires covered with a tarpaulin. Later on, we bought large net bags that we stuffed with foam rubber remnants that were given to us in lieu of throwing them away.

—Jim Tate

In 1974 the McCall Field House was built. It was large enough for one tennis and two basketball courts, and it also included a weight room, coaches' offices, storage space, and five locker rooms with showers. With the completion of this facility, the administration had made its commitment to athletics clear.

THE RICHARD H. FURMAN
Family

After fifty years, CCES is educating second and third-generation students. Returning families are a great source of pride because they validate the purposes and methods of the School. Clearly, these returning alumni want for their children a school experience similar to their own. One such family is the **Richard H. Furman** family.

Richard came to CCES from 1966–68, when the School ended at ninth grade. He earned the Citizenship Award all three years and participated in nearly every available sport. Richard's wife, Nancy Yeargin Furman '73, enrolled in 1970 and became a legendary tennis player who went on to compete at Wimbledon. She too earned the Citizenship Award in grades 10–12 and was secretary/treasurer of the student body as a senior.

In time, the Furman children, **Rick '07**, **Robert '09**, and **Sitton '15**, enrolled at CCES, each one excelling academically and athletically in his or her own way. Rick was, among other distinctions, a National Merit Semifinalist, a Vestry member in grades 10–12, All-State in soccer, and All-Region in football. Furman University awarded him both its prestigious Hollingsworth Scholarship and a football scholarship. Robert's awards included being named All-State and All-Region in both soccer and football. Robert also participated in Youth in Government in grades 10–12 and demonstrated an unexpected ability to sing in the Upper School Christmas Cabaret.

The youngest Furman, Sitton, has already earned distinction among her Middle School classmates for her abilities in tennis, soccer, and basketball.

Yet, even with their perennial success in sports, the Furmans value the spiritual and academic education at CCES as much as its athletic opportunities. In 2003 Nancy told an audience:

> *We are all aware that, in the pursuit of excellence, not all A's will be made, not every game or match will be won, not every theater performance will be performed to perfection, but to have the opportunity to pursue excellence is victory in itself. The high expectations and standards at CCES have been key for our children, who, like all children, have different gifts. Richard and I have seen CCES encourage and stretch them beyond their comfort zones in and out of the classroom. And we are thankful they have had the opportunity to attend.*

In 2006 Nancy spoke again at the dedication of the Cavalier Training Center. She held up a framed photo of what she prized most in the School's athletic program. It was not a picture of a state championship team celebrating a victory; rather, it showed the football team huddled together in prayer. Athletics, she reminded the audience, is one piece of a CCES education, but by no means the most important one.

Left, The unequalled 1978 championship football team.

Below, John Kittredge '75, Coach Jim Tate, and Rick Knight '74 during the 1974 football season. In 2006 Kittredge inducted Knight into the CCES Sports Hall of Fame.

Left, Teachers, the Lower School Director, even clergy have often doubled as coaches at CCES. In 1978 the IA State Championship football coaching staff included, *kneeling, left to right,* Father Crowther, Coach Harry Sprouse, and Coach Jerry Powell. *Standing, from left,* Lower School Director David Williams and Foreign Language Chair Chris Hearon.

Showing their Cavalier spirit at an athletic event are, *standing from left*, Missy Park '80, Greg Hendershot '81, Mike Sierra '82, Frank O'Brien '82, Billy Richardson '81, and Derrick Quattlebaum '82. Seated in the foreground is Laurie Siminski '81.

A group of Middle School girls shows their school spirit. Today, with all three divisions on the Cavalier Campus, even Lower School students participate in spirit events, including what one youngster called "a pepper rally."

Missy Park '80

At a time when women's sports were not supported at many schools nationally, Lillian (Missy) Hunter Park '80 was an accomplished athlete who lettered in six sports: tennis, basketball, track, volleyball, field hockey, and softball. But Missy was intent on more than just athletic success. She was also a distinguished student who became a National Merit Scholarship Semifinalist and earned the Era Sigma Phi Latin Award. Such achievement, especially in Latin and Science, led to her acceptance to Yale University.

Missy's passion for sports continued through college. After graduating from Yale, she served briefly as an assistant basketball coach at both Harvard and Yale. But she chose not to build a lifelong career for herself as either athlete or coach. Instead, relying as much on her keen intelligence as on her love of sport, she set about building and managing a business that catered to the athletic dreams of women. Today Missy is President and CEO of Title Nine, Inc., a $10-million-a-year catalog and retail business that offers clothing for female athletes.

Missy credits the opportunities she enjoyed at CCES for shaping her character and her success. Memories of making a free throw in front of an expectant crowd gave her mental strength and perseverance. "We got attention from the School and validation in what we accomplished," Missy said. It was the chance to pursue both academics and athletics with equal passion that ultimately made a difference in Missy's life.

The 1981 girls tennis championship team. *Front row, left to right*, Gwinn Earle '85, Rae Rogers '83, Donna Pazdan '82, and Allison Betette '82. *Back row,* Anne Bailey '82, Laura Cochran '83, Martha Wood '82, and Bonnie Berry '81.

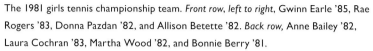

The 1998–99 boys tennis team initiated an eight-year winning streak of state championships.

The 2008–09 girls basketball team was the first ever to win a state championship.

Navy Blue to Cavalier Blue,

BY JOHN KITTREDGE '75

When I was in seventh grade, a popular history teacher and coach, **Mike Stevenson** (1963–69) left CCES mid-year for another school. A fellow by the name of Jim Tate was hired to replace Coach Stevenson. Up to this point, the School colors were navy blue and white, I believe by default – the school basketball team originally used the Church's uniforms and warm-ups. If it was good enough for the Church, it was good enough for the School.

That changed with the arrival of Coach Tate, who [was] a graduate of The Citadel. To say Coach Tate is fond of his *alma mater* would be an understatement. He wasted little time in changing the school colors to light blue and white. There was no resistance, for there was no compelling attachment to navy blue. That light blue is frequently referred to as "Carolina blue," but Coach Tate made it clear that the color [was] "Citadel blue," which through the years became known as "Cavalier blue."

Beginning in 2000–2001, Coach David Wilcox has led nine consecutive boys soccer teams to the state championship.

The 2001 girls soccer team has been the only one to win the state championship in CCES history.

In 1975 CCES joined the South Carolina High School Athletic Association (SCHSA) Class A Division in order to compete on a consistently higher level. Schools within the Carolinas Athletic Association (CAA), of which it had been part, were not only fewer in number, but also were spread too far around both Carolinas. Now CCES could test its ability against larger, varied, and closer opponents. Moreover, there would be more opportunities for athletes with aspirations to play at the college level.

Almost immediately, two CCES teams proved their ability to succeed in the new league. In 1976 the boys golf and varsity tennis teams won state championship titles, followed by a girls tennis championship the next year. It was the start of a more competitive era in CCES athletics.

The boys varsity tennis team was coached by the fiery, pipe-smoking Pete Cooper (1971–79), a former tennis player at The Citadel, who was then Upper School Director. His love for the game and his devotion to his players fostered exceptional passion on the tennis and basketball courts. The 1974 *Hellenian* summarized the JV basketball season with "Coach Pete Cooper went the whole season without drawing a technical until the final game!"

Latin teacher Chris Hearon followed Cooper as varsity tennis coach. Although his style was more reserved than Cooper's, he led the team to another winning streak of five consecutive championships. His record even caught the attention of *The Greenville News Piedmont,* which predicted, "… as long as the sun is shining, and Prince is making tennis racquets, Christ Church will win in tennis."

Coaches **Jerry Knight** (1974–77) and **Harry Sprouse** (1976–89) developed the 1977 state championship football team. Both men knew how to balance grit with humor, and they became lifelong mentors to many players.

In 2009 Jay Jackson '05 was pitching for Chicago Cubs Double-A Team, the Tennessee Smokies. He is one of two CCES athletes to turn pro. Mills Ariail '91 played NFL football for the Seattle Seahawks. Photo credit: *The Greenville News.*

Jerry got more out of his athletes than anyone thought possible, including the athletes themselves. No matter what the sport, Jerry's practices were always well-structured. We ran drills until we could execute the plays without thinking about them. And when we weren't running drills, we were simply running….

Rasmi Gamble '02 holds two CCES basketball records: 2,418 career points scored and 1,315 rebounds. In 2006 his basketball jersey was retired and now hangs with Mills Ariail's football jersey, retired in 1995, and Abby Simon Lyle's volleyball jersey, retired in 2008.

Jerry also had a nickname for every player, and they weren't just your standard nicknames. Some names took more time for Jerry to develop than others, like a fine wine. But oh, when he came up with one, it was usually a doozy, and it showed Jerry really knew his players.

—Glenn Goodwin '77

After the 70s, there was a lull in terms of championships teams. There were certainly many winning seasons and much to celebrate each year, but the big trophies seemed out of reach for nearly two decades.

At their induction in 1999 into the CCES Sports Hall of Fame, *from left,* Coach Linda Reeves, Donny Harrison '79, and Missy Park '80.

Today, however, state championships are almost routine. Since 1997, CCES has won thirty-two South Carolina High School League (SCHSL) state championships. The varsity boys and girls tennis and boys golf teams have resumed their former reign in the state, and boys soccer has also established itself as a consistent state champion. Boys and girls cross country teams have won several state championships, and girls volleyball, soccer, basketball, and track teams have each earned championship trophies in the last decade.

Every year beginning in 1993 CCES has won the Wachovia Cup, an award now known as the Athletic Director's Cup. It is given in each division to "the most outstanding athletic program in South Carolina," based on team records and post-season results. Ashley Haskins (1987–2008), **Travis Perry** (2005–08), and **R. J. Beach** (1994–present), recent athletic directors, deserve much credit for elevating the athletic program. Haskins began as a Lower School P.E. instructor and was named Athletic Director in 1998 because of his enthusiastic and positive leadership. In 2005 Perry was asked to concentrate on

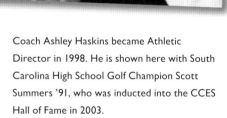

Coach Ashley Haskins became Athletic Director in 1998. He is shown here with South Carolina High School Golf Champion Scott Summers '91, who was inducted into the CCES Hall of Fame in 2003.

Athletic Director Pete Cooper with Homecoming Queen Lauren Steinman '77.

administering the program and expanding coaching and physical resources. Following Perry, Beach has led the athletic program to further prominence, guiding many outstanding athletes to play at the collegiate level.

Even with this expanding program, the primary purpose of CCES athletics remained consistent with its origins: to benefit as many participants as possible, regardless of previous experience or training. "I define success in terms of how close a team comes to reaching its potential," said Beach in 2008. Today, a formal statement of the School's athletic philosophy emphasizes that the sports program encompasses far more than victory on the field or on the court:

> *Christ Church Episcopal School believes that all aspects of our student's well-being are important and that many important lessons are taught through an athletic experience. The goal of coaches and teachers is identical: to help young people reach their fullest potential….We strive to offer our students, who vary in their athletic interest and ability, quality programs that appropriately challenge them to stretch their limits of endurance, and fosters self-discipline, loyalty, self-confidence, leadership, cooperation, and sportsmanship….CCES believes that athletics provide opportunities to shape students' character and self-awareness.*

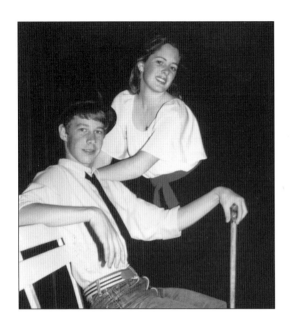

Darrell Jervey '82, as a particularly benign-looking Devil, and Susan Fowler '81, as Lola, in the 1980 Upper School production of *Damn Yankees*.

THE ARTS

In August 1959, recognizing that a classical education included an understanding and appreciation of the arts, Roberts hired Ruth Watson to teach music and French. Despite budget and space constraints, the programs quickly became an integral part of the curriculum.

Watson held music class in an empty, oversized broom closet to the right of Finley Hall's front doors, where she also composed musicals. Her successor was **Bob Powell** (1969–99), an accomplished organist at Christ Church and well-known composer of liturgical music. He tried to use a balcony room overlooking the gymnasium as a classroom but wound up propping a

Students triumph over then-sixth-form teacher Rufus Bethea, who played the Giant in Ruth Watson's 1960s production of *Jack and the Magic Beanstalk*. When he retired from the School, students published a tribute to Bethea, calling him "a giant in any endeavor."

mattress against the door to muffle the noise below. "It was the sound of kids' feet banging against the radiators where they sat waiting to play that was nearly deafening," said **Kay Quinn**, Lower School art instructor (1970–80), who had also attempted to teach from that same room. Quinn was inventive and resourceful. She found ways to stretch her students, such as taking them outdoors to rub headstones in the cemetery or sketch Markley Chapel. She taught pottery even though the kiln was hidden behind the stage and her water source was in the janitor's closet. For the Primers, she set up six large tables daily, each with different media, to keep them engaged.

The Cavalier Players have performed the ever-popular *Sound of Music* in 1976, 1993, and 2007. Here, photos from the 1993 and 2007 productions.

In 1971 **Jourdan Newton McFee** (1971–74) started a Drama Club as an extension of the Upper School English Department. Her budget was minimal, supplies nonexistent, and her classroom undefined. Yet in her first year she managed to direct two Broadway shows, performing them on the Finley Hall stage downtown.

I don't know how we did it, but we had a fabulous set. We had pipes and barrels and even a balcony for the ghetto setting in The Me Nobody Knows. We also had a band that Mr. Powell helped direct. The actors helped, the parents helped…nobody took anything for granted and people loved it. Parents still come up to me today to tell me how much the plays meant to their child.

—Jourdan McFee

By 1975 the Upper School had a designated Fine Arts Department. **Sue Russell** (1973–77) taught watercolor, oil, and acrylic classes, as well as sculpting, graphic design, and ceramics. **Marilyn Kimbell** (1974–78) joined the Music

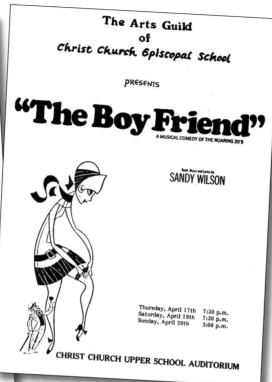

Department and directed programs for Parents Night, Christmas, Lower School assemblies, chapel services, and school plays. Under the able direction of **Karen Clark** (1974–2000), the English Department offered a drama elective for grades 10–12 that performed such plays as *Cheaper By the Dozen*. There was even a course in film-making.

Pam Robinson (1979–86) followed Kimbell as head of Upper School music. Single-handedly, she directed one memorable musical after another, shaping students such as Lynn McColl '81, who called Robinson "the most inspiring directress for whom I ever worked." Among her repertoire were *Oliver, Damn Yankees, Amahl and the Night Visitors* (in which **Edwin McCain '88** played Amahl), and *Oklahoma*.

I remember how much fun it was to work with Pam Robinson, how she seemed to do a million things at once and still make everyone feel she was watching out for them and concerned for their happiness…the privilege of having a starring role as a seventh-grader in the high school play with little voice and no clue what to do on stage, but doing it anyway…that great song, "Who Will Buy" that I still sing to myself sometimes…how much fun it was… Did I say that already?

—Jonathan Shoemaker '85 (Oliver)

Left, The program from the 1994 production of *Oliver*. Mary Echols '81, who appeared in the 1979 production, remembered, "It was the first time I had had a principal role in a school production… When my character was killed, the lights were to be turned off, to be turned on after I exited the stage. However, after each performance the lights came up too soon; it was very obvious to the audience that I was alive and well."

Right, The program from Molly (Hoffman) Aiken's first CCES production in 1985.

In 1981 **W. G. Anderson** and **Dr.** and **Mrs. E. D. Jervey** donated thirty-seven Malmark English handbells, and Chris Hearon's Cavaltones barbershop quartet, comprised largely of varsity football players, released an album. The enthusiasm and energy among students wanting to participate bubbled over, but still the arts programs had neither continuity nor satisfactory budgets.

In 1985 **Susanne Abrams** (1985–present) and **Molly Hoffman Aiken** (1985–present) joined the faculty to teach art and music respectively. Both women were accomplished artists, and both envisioned broader programs that would better prepare students for artistic careers. The question was whether or not the School could support their ambitious goals.

Working collaboratively in groups, students in Alice (Munn) Ballard's 1997 art classes designed and painted this tile mural representing CCES activities. Art students in each division have participated in similar projects, greatly enhancing the school environment.

Above, Susanne Abrams began teaching art to CCES students in 1985. Here, she helps a student working on a clay sculpture during an artist's residency by Marsha Kennedy '95. Visiting artists enrich the fine arts curriculum by exposing students to new media, artistic styles, and projects. *Left,* In 2005–06 CCES helped bring ceramicist Lin Yung here from China to teach traditional Chinese brush painting techniques on paper and ceramics.

The music program often includes community performances such as this Christmas concert led by Lower School music teacher Rita Hughes at the Hyatt in downtown Greenville.

Our budgets were spare, although the School supported us as best it could. Once, when I spent $11 to have my lessons typed for my students, Jim Rumrill called me into his office to question the expense! We did our best to work within our spare budgets, and we had to be very resourceful. Parents were immensely supportive. Some donated materials, such as the family of Craig Ragsdale '99, whose printing business generously supplied us with paper. But it was the Arts Guild that has made all the difference to our programs. When I came to the School, I had no place to display the students' work. The Arts Guild bought portable panels so that I could set up periodic displays in the Upper School commons. Next, they purchased lights, so we could finally see the art! Then they provided funding to frame the top 10-12 artworks each year for the CCES Permanent Collection. Their sponsorship of the Visiting Artist program has allowed us to venture into new projects and obtain new materials for them. Whenever we have needed something over and above what our budget could provide, the Arts Guild has helped us. Our arts programs have grown, in large measure, because of their support.

—Susanne Abrams

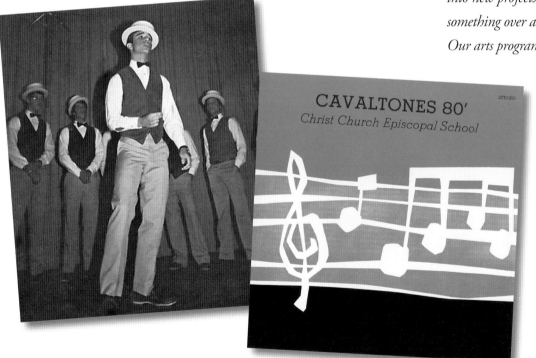

The Arts Guild has been similarly supportive of the CCES music and drama programs.

In 1987 CCES hired **Rita Hughes** (1987–2004) to teach Lower School music along with Bob Powell. Hughes immediately began a handbell choir using the forgotten Malmark bells. She and Lower School art teacher **Kathy Wood** (1984–95) exposed students to a variety of genres to broaden the curriculum.

This photo was taken from the jacket of the Cavaltones' LP record issued in 1980. The group, led by faculty advisor Chris Hearon, performed not only at school functions but also at public venues in Greenville and Charleston.

Left, With the help of the Arts Guild, Molly Hoffman Aiken's musical productions gained a reputation for professional sets, elaborate costumes—and great voices. This photo is from the 1999 production of *Cinderella.*

Above, Cinderella (Elizabeth Provence '01) and her evil stepsisters (*from left,* Laurie Mason' 01, Ashley Rudisill '01, and Ana Ortega '01) in a scene from Sondheim's *Into the Woods,* performed in spring 2001 at CCES, and reprised that summer at the International Fringe Festival in Edinburgh.

Left, CCES began staging Renaissance madrigals every three years in the early 80s. Performed in Markley Chapel, they featured period costumes, dances, and song, and culminated in an elaborate feast fit for a king. Both faculty and students participated in the madrigals. Here, the cast from the 1983 production.

With large casts, the annual Middle School musicals, such as this 2008 production of *Annie*, give many students the experience to go on to more demanding dramatic and musical productions in the Upper School. Photo credit: Dara Productions.

Then, in the 1990s and 2000s, several forces worked together to bolster the arts program. First, the addition of a new Middle School building on campus in 1995 created a need for music and art directors in that division. All along there had been numerous dedicated teachers for the Upper and Lower Schools, but there had been little effort toward creating a continuum of skills from one grade level to the next. Now, with three distinct divisions together on one campus, the time was right to develop a comprehensive, interconnected curriculum beginning in Primer and continuing through grade 12.

Secondly, with new buildings came studios that could accommodate additional programs, such as graphic arts, sculpture, and photography. Thirdly, there was a faculty of highly skilled, practicing artists in place for each division. It could attract students inclined to pursue artistic interests in earnest.

By 2003 the arts programs had become so important to the School's identity that the board, under Chair Frances Ellison, added the phrase "vibrant arts," along with "strong academics" and "comprehensive athletics," to the CCES mission statement. It was an official acknowledgement of how much the arts programs had advanced.

Today it is obvious to any campus visitor that the School values student artwork. The Upper School art gallery regularly rotates exhibits of student landscapes, self-portraits, photography, pottery, and sculpture as well as projects that complement the academic curriculum. Student-designed posters are displayed throughout the halls to advertise musical and dramatic productions. Under the guidance of **Alice (Munn) Ballard** (1996–present) and **Marilyn (Wood) Mullinax** (1995–present), tile murals, handmade quilts, and brightly painted wooden animals adorn the Middle and Lower School buildings. The annual Lower and Middle School art fairs reveal skill and versatility in even the youngest students.

When the International Fringe Festival in Edinburgh, Scotland, invited CCES to perform in summer 2005, Molly (Hoffman) Aiken conceived, wrote, composed, and directed a musical production just for the occasion. Her students offered four world-premiere performances of *Hats: A Musical Tribute to Scottish Colourist John Duncan Fergusson.*

Now, many extra-curricular opportunities exist in the fine arts. There are nine separate choral groups in the three divisions, including a handbell choir in the Lower School; band and orchestra; a strings program starting in fourth grade; private instruction in guitar, piano, and drums; visiting authors, artists, and musicians funded by the Arts Guild; annual Middle and Upper School concerts and musical productions; and spring and fall drama productions in the Upper School.

Among the most popular extra-curricular opportunities are the Lower, Middle, and Upper School plays. Ambitious productions, such as the Upper School performance of *Les Miserable* in 2005, electrify audiences with their professionalism, and they enable students to taste success on stage or behind the scenes.

The arts program expanded in the new Upper School with the addition of a graphic arts program. Here, Amanda Gavron '04 with a digital portrait.

Much credit for these outstanding productions belongs to Molly Aiken. With a BFA in vocal music from Tulane University, a master's degree in music from Converse, and experience in off-Broadway musical theater, she was able to choreograph and orchestrate many musicals that had never before been tried. Together with Middle School Director **Tina Batchelder-Schwab** (2007–present), and Lower School Director **Joy Hughes** (1994–present), the current faculty is exceptional.

> *I can genuinely say that Molly [Hoffman Aiken] has been the wings beneath me. She taught me so many things of which she is not even aware. She taught me to fly. That is what makes her the incredible teacher she is.*
>
> —Elizabeth Provence '01

One affirmation of the arts program is the number of students who have gone on to pursue an arts degree or career following graduation. **Marsha Kennedy '95** is a lawyer and a professional painter and sculptor working to empower Western African communities. **Jessica Green '98**, a graphic artist in New York City, said, "I owe it all to Susanne Abrams. I had an amazing art experience at CCES." **Alex Ritter '03**, whose interest in sound engineering blossomed under drama teacher **David Sims** (2000–present), now tours as a professional sound engineer with bands such as Coldplay, Hootie and the Blowfish, and Lynyrd Skynyrd.

LEADERSHIP, PUBLICATIONS, AND CLUBS

The very first administrators understood the value of giving students the chance to prove themselves outside the classroom. By 1965 there was a student government, four clubs, the *Delphian* magazine, the *Hellenian* yearbook, and two newspapers open to anyone interested.

Leadership

Today leadership begins in earnest in the fourth grade. As the oldest students in the Lower School, they are able to become safety patrols, acolytes, and Primer Book Buddies. They deliver Meals-on-Wheels and collect canned goods for United Ministries and the Project Host Soup Kitchen. Such experiences prepare them for Middle School, when Student Council provides a new opportunity for leadership.

The Middle School Student Council dates back to 1974, when Allen Bray decided it was necessary to give more responsibility to students in grades 7, 8, and 9. That year, Upper School Student Body President **Allen Gibson '75** implemented a new School constitution that called for separate Middle and Upper School councils. Each council had five committees made up of elected members who would work on such matters such as fundraising or beautification. Almost from the beginning, this structure created a sense of ownership in the School among students. It became an honor to be part of either council making decisions on behalf of others.

A similar structure continues today, although there are no longer separate committees within the two councils. Instead, the president, vice president, and secretary/treasurer meet with student representatives from each grade to plan major events such as Homecoming and Spring Fling. In the Middle School, students learn about leadership by working with faculty advisors. But by the time students reach the Upper School, the student government has unusual latitude. "When the Upper School Director says, 'Plan Homecoming,' we plan it. The good thing about Christ Church is the freedom you have to lead," said **Smyth McKissick '08**, who served as 2007– 08 Upper School Student Council President.

The Honor Council is another student group with a central role. In an environment where honesty and integrity are paramount, the Honor Council chair shoulders the responsibility of investigating violations of the Honor Code and recommending disciplinary actions. The chair and the council must be able to uphold a core value system even when it conflicts with popular thinking. Such positions of authority at a young age tend to leave lasting impressions. Former Honor Council Chairman **Travis McElveen '07** said of his experience, "I am leaving CCES with leadership skills I will use throughout my life."

Student government positions are incubators for leadership skills. In this photo from the 1967 *Hellenian,* Headmaster Bethea sits with student government representatives. Front right is Knox White, whose leadership as Greenville's mayor since 1995 has had a marked impact on the city.

Publications

School publications have long provided an outlet for creative expression, as well as training in managing people. The first *Athenian* magazine combined news and poetry. It had the appearance of a typed church bulletin with over-inked periods and semi-colons. Guthrie introduced it in November 1959:

It is with pardonable pride, I hope, that we present our first literary effort in our news magazine, The Athenian. *Increasingly, this will become the medium of our students. Although we felt a need of a newspaper for the school, we recognize that equally important is the fact that our students need stimulation for creative writing, and who can be interested in writing unless he has hope of it being published?*

In time, *The Athenian* evolved into two separate publications. The *Delphian* literary magazine began in 1963, and school newspapers began in 1965. The *Hellenian*, as it was known from the first year, remained a separate endeavor for students and faculty advisors.

In 1969 students published the first *Cavalier Express*. Editor **Nancy Page '71** declared, "Often student newspapers are either intentionally or by design vehicles for the official point of view of the school administration. We are determined that this will not happen to this newspaper. It will be written strictly by students – for students." Thirty-five years later her daughter **Emily Bridges '08** became editor of a longer, more sophisticated *Cavalier Express*, and the original editorial policy had not changed.

Right, A page from the first issue of The Athenian, published in the fall of 1959. This mimeographed literary "magazine" evolved into today's award-winning Delphian (below), which is produced as a for-credit academic class.

The staff of the first *Cavalier Express*. In the foreground is editor Nancy Page '71.

The current *Delphian*, *Hellenian*, and *Cavalier Express* only faintly resemble their former incarnations. The *Hellenian* is typically more than 300 pages, covering a myriad of student activities throughout the year. The *Delphian* is now a sophisticated, award-winning collection of high school creative writing, photography, and artwork. And the *Cavalier Express*, formerly a simple black-and-white publication with handwritten headlines, is now a colorful newspaper laid out by students using special software. Once extra-curricular activities, these publications have become elective classes for the time they require.

Naming the School Newspaper

BY JOHN KITTREDGE '75

When I was in junior high, it was decided that we would have a school newspaper. (Calling it a newspaper in the early years was quite a stretch.) There was a contest to name the newspaper. I came up with the name *Cavalier Express*. I was so proud of the name that I made the mistake of telling several people of my entry in the contest. The day came to announce the winner, and there were two entries for the *Cavalier Express* – me and a classmate. I, of course, knew my entry had been stolen and I demanded justice. I wanted the grand prize. My nefarious classmate and I were summoned to Headmaster Rufus Bethea's office, whereupon the classmate promptly wilted and confessed to the felony of copying my entry of *Cavalier Express*. I was declared the winner, entitling me to the grand prize.

Top of the heap: John Kittredge '75 at the top of this group of second-grade boys in 1965. Today he is a South Carolina Supreme Court judge.

The grand prize was a free subscription for the remainder of the school year. Each copy was five cents. Because sales were less than brisk, it was decided after a couple of months just to give them away. What a grand prize.

William (Billy) Marr Campbell III

'78

A CCES student for only four years, **Billy Campbell** nonetheless left a lasting mark on the School. He was the consummate "all-American" boy eager to take part in every sport, club, and leadership opportunity available.

Billy first joined the *Cavalier Express*, the Pep Club, and football and basketball teams in ninth grade. The following year he played baseball, became a founding member of the Block C Club, and was All-Conference in basketball. His junior year he was All-Conference in basketball and football, a student representative to the Booster Club, a member of Student Council, and an acolyte. By his senior year, Billy was the captain of the varsity football and basketball teams, a member of the Honor Council, and Head Acolyte.

Campbell enrolled at Harvard University in the fall of 1978. Following graduation from college, he spent a year as a Rotary Scholar at the Chinese University of Hong Kong and toured the country as a member of their basketball team. Afterwards, he returned to Harvard for an MBA. One snowy day during his final semester of business school, Billy trudged to a marketing class where he unexpectedly met the CEO of Capital Cities/ABC. Within weeks of the encounter, he had a job in Los Angeles as a "bridge between the 'creatives' and the 'suits,'" Campbell said. It was the start of a felicitous career.

In 2008 Billy returned to CCES to speak to Middle and Upper School students about his thirty-year odyssey since graduation. In characteristically down-to-earth style, he recalled sitting where his audience sat and wondering where "my life would take me." He talked of the importance of overcoming adversity and how winning the state championship in football his senior year at CCES had "been a tremendous source of pride and confidence throughout my life.... There is not a day that passes that I don't think about that accomplishment and get a big smile on my face," he said. It was a significant statement from the man who had been President of Discovery Networks USA and President and CEO of Panavision.

Billy Campbell '78, *right,* then President of Discovery Networks US, talks with newscaster Ted Koppel during a presentation of *Up Front* in 2006.

Perhaps Billy Campbell came into the world an optimist, but CCES gave him the foundation to pursue his most ambitious dreams. It was a "warm and comforting environment where the faculty made every effort to accommodate the students," Campbell said. His memories of walking down the bank to football games on chilly Friday nights or studying in the commons have remained vivid even after conquering the multi-billion dollar entertainment industry in the USA and abroad. "There is no question, [CCES] is part of my DNA," he said.

Clubs

Clubs provide another avenue for involvement. Although they have always been part of school life, they have evolved and changed over time.

In 1965 there was a Latin Club, Pep Club, Drama Club, and Science Club. The groups met periodically to select leaders and plan events. Over the years, the number of clubs grew to include a Glee Club, Outdoors Club, Spanish Club, and French Club, among others.

In some cases, the faculty initiated and even participated in clubs. Jim Tate organized the Block C Club "to act as a bridge between coaches and athletes" who had lettered in a varsity sport. In 1975 the Madrigal Group was formed for students and faculty interested in singing in an advanced chorus.

Throughout the School's history, students themselves have also organized clubs with permission. The Middle School Cheerleading Club, the Middle School Soccer Club, the Shag Club, and a Fencing Club founded by **John Freeman '06** are examples of student initiatives that have come and gone as interest has waxed and waned. Some, such as the Blue Belles founded in 1997 by **Kemper LeCroy '99**, continue to flourish.

A glorious spring day in 2002 brought the Improv Club outdoors to perform.

Today clubs beginning in Middle School center around books, academic competitions, volunteerism, Lego Robotics, environmental awareness, art, sports, foreign language, choral singing, Model United Nations, and Bible studies. But it is an ever-evolving list that reflects the ever-changing interests of the student body.

Opportunities for growth abound at CCES. They are a part of the School's mission to provide an environment in which students can develop to their full potential. Here there is an underlying belief that every child has unique talents waiting to surface. Sometimes these co-curricular experiences will determine a student's direction in life. In other cases, they will merely fade into memory. Either way, they become part of the journey that shapes character and enhances lives.

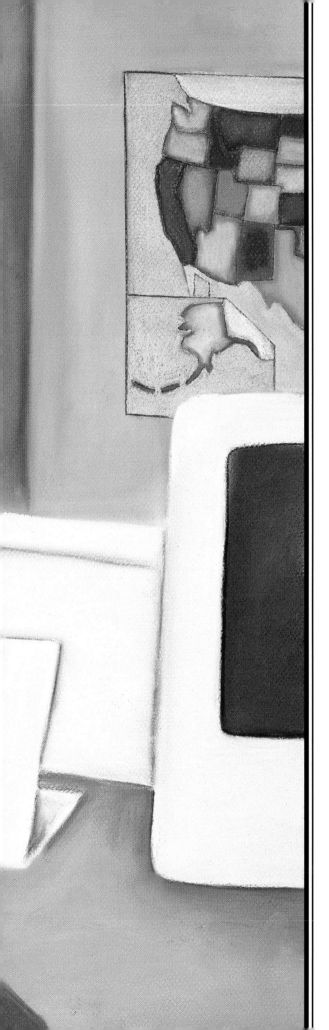

The Journey Continues

Much as a traveler might keep a journal to record insights and memories, students from the Class of 2009 have penned their own thoughts about a CCES education in this last chapter of our history. Their comments provide a snapshot of the School fifty years after it was founded. Will these observations seem out of date in another fifty years? Probably. We cannot know where the educational terrain may lead in the future. All we know is that it will continue to change. And then, as now, we believe that the journey will be its own reward.

CHAPTER

7

CCES TODAY

In the fall of 2008 **Barbara Carter** assigned members of her senior English class the task of describing a particularly meaningful part of their day. The excerpts that follow reveal an energetic, thoughtful, and involved student population not so different from the first students who came in 1959.

> *It goes without saying that the academics at CCES are very stringent. Regardless of whether we are talking about freshman biology and its related projects, or chemistry and the labs that go hand-in-hand with that discipline, or AB and BC calculus, or AP Modern European History, or AP English, or Senior Thesis, or (in more recent years) IB Psychology, or the IB Extended Essay, the expectations are at the highest level, the students have learned how to function in such an environment, and they regularly produce truly excellent work. We send our students to the finest colleges and universities in the country, and they have been more than successful wherever they have gone. So, when one asks our students about their "day in the life of CCES," they usually turn to the many other things that accompany their academics because, for them, superior academic expectations are a given.*

—Barbara Carter, English Department Chair

Students' passion for athletics can be seen in the fact that seven seniors, shown here with their families, announced their intentions to play college sports in 2009.

EARLY MORNING

For some, the morning is a crucial time of day. It is the last chance to perfect an assignment or memorize a chemical formula before a test. For others, it provides the only opportunity for music lessons, play practice, or club meetings before classwork and athletics begin. One student begins her day with the Blue Belles:

Getting to school at 7:30 a.m. isn't easy for any teenager, especially for Christ Church students already busy with school, sports, and other activities. However, this is what the 10-12 girls that make up the Blue Belles have been doing every Monday and Thursday morning for the past several years. [Having begun] as a senior thesis project, Blue Belles is now a CCES tradition. Today, there are certain school-wide occasions where we are expected to sing, including Convocation, football games, basketball games, Grandparents' Day, Senior Chapel, and Awards Night. Like the School itself, Blue Belles represent both change and continuation. As senior leaders this year, we seek to keep Blue Belles alive and to pass the songs on to the next generation.

—Janice Hu '09

The Blue Belles performing at Awards Night 2009.

THE SCHOOL DAY

The school day begins at 8:10 and ends at 3:35. During that time, there are eight periods and a thirty-five-minute lunch break beginning at 12:43. Twice a week, on Mondays and Wednesdays, students attend chapel services, receiving Holy Communion on Wednesdays.

Some students perform during chapel services:

It is 6:30 Wednesday morning when my alarm goes off. I pull on my button-up shirt and put that noose around my neck that most people call a tie. After getting ready, I grab my bass and my books and head to school. Before I go to chapel, however, I must first go to my locker and get my bass. This after all is the reason I am going to chapel so early in the first place: I am a musician. This makes it so that chapel day is always a very interesting day for me.

—Eric Evert '09

Another reflects on the significance of Wednesday morning chapel:

Chapel services are essentially a weekly coming together of the School as a community. This calm time for reflection is important for the students to have every week, when the rest of the week seems to be hectic and stressful. Each week, Father Richard [Grimball] reminds us that we are loved and prayed for; this message is always very encouraging as we head off to face another challenging week.

—Chelsea Lawdahl '09

Production of the *Cavalier Express* used to take place after school, but it has now become so demanding that it is an academic class. The newspaper staff takes pride in their work:

I am the Co-Editor-in-Chief of the Cavalier Express, *the school newspaper, where there is always a pressing matter. But I take a great deal of comfort in the fact that we have a self-motivated staff. They never have to be asked to do something twice. This past Halloween I was particularly impressed. The annual Primer Halloween parade was walking through the Upper School, and I couldn't remember whether we had assigned any cameras to the event. I was pleasantly surprised to learn [later] that many excellent pictures had been taken without my even asking. Through all the ups and downs of journalism, the feeling of accomplishment when the paper is finally printed makes it all worth it.*

—Alex Wagner '09

THE ACADEMIC DAY

Students follow their academic schedules, moving from class to class. But the academic day offers many additional experiences, such as Student Council meetings and those very welcome "free periods."

It's Tuesday, just after X period, and the bell rings. **Ms. [Sara] Allison** *[Upper School Administrative Assistant] announces lunch and that the Student Council will meet in the Private Dining Room. Council members from each grade file into the dining room. Student Council advisors follow, and with the crunching noises of lunch in the background, the meeting begins. We have chosen our Homecoming theme, "The Blue Night," a play on the recent Batman movie. However, there is still much work to do. Each project goes into so much more detail than anyone could imagine. What color will the t-shirt be? Who will design it? How will people order the shirt? How much money will we charge? Who will distribute the shirts once they come in? It's the behind-the-scenes work we do that make our meetings busy yet full of fun and laughter. This year's Homecoming was better than any other I had ever experienced. As a fund-raiser, Student Council chose to raise money for Maggie's School in Kenya in memory of* **Maggie McLeod '05,** *who died tragically in a car accident. By the end of the week, the CCES high school raised $5,000 to buy toilets for Maggie's School. What a great cause and a great week!*

—Jennings Johnstone '09

"Downtime" is important too:

Free periods: those magical periods in which students have no obligations and no place they have to be. In theory, they are awesome. The idea of doing whatever you want thrills the underclassmen. However, as students move up in the Upper School, they begin to grasp the importance of free periods. They no longer become a time for relaxation and fun. They become a necessity.... Students are swamped with projects, essays, and homework assignments. Not to mention that most participate in time-consuming after-school activities. Free periods can be used as a time to do homework, to cram for tests, or, in rare cases, to catch up on sleep.... They are, without a doubt, vital to a majority of the students.

—Reid Polstra '09

Students appreciate their freedom and responsibility:

The Senior Lounge is a terrific privilege that CCES offers. It provides seniors with fun and comfort, but it teaches responsibility at the same time. It is another thing that makes Christ Church different from other schools. The trust that the faculty has in the students here to manage their time well and maintain the Senior Lounge is great. The Christ Church community is like a family where everyone trusts each other.

—Ian Conits '09

The variety and excitement of a day at CCES can be found in unexpected places:

*Only at CCES can you have an "80s Day" in Physical Education for absolutely no reason. During my freshman year, my PE class felt the need for one. Coach [**Sally Shurtz**] Pielou was kind enough to allow us this day of tacky outfits for our last class. My memory of this day is not meant to say that our school is random, rather to say that it is varied. Only days before "80s Day," we were learning CPR. Only here can a member of the football team be a member of the Carolina Youth Symphony or a girly girl become part of the Outdoors Club. Only here are students given the chance and flexibility to pursue any dream.*

—Kate Stewart '09

AFTER SCHOOL

When the bell rings at 3:35 p.m., students disperse, often only to return later. A large percentage of Upper School students participate in athletics for at least one season. Aside from athletics, there are fall and spring musical productions, school publications, art shows, and clubs. These activities not only promote friendships and school spirit; they also awaken students to undiscovered talents.

School athletics are important to many students:

The unique tradition of girls field hockey continues.

Field hockey has deep roots at CCES. Though some things have drastically changed over the years, some things – the good things – have never changed. The pleated skirts, long bus rides to North Carolina, and most importantly, the camaraderie developed throughout the season, are all things that come from playing field hockey at CCES.

—Holly McKissick '09

Workouts in the Cavalier Training Center also become after-school activities. Situated at the far end of the Carson Stadium, this building draws students with an atmosphere and energy all its own.

You can already hear it as you approach the door – the sounds of loud music and weights crashing to the ground, often followed by a hyped-up yell. As you enter, those sounds are intensified, along with the sweaty smell of young athletes hard at work in the Cavalier Training Center. For me, this place is almost sacred. Being here with my team motivates me as a football team captain to push myself and show the younger guys what it means to be a Cavalier. No matter if it is 100 degrees outside and all the doors to the Center are open, you can find the football team here. Or if the season has just ended on Friday, you can find the football team here Monday morning. It is here among our coaches and teammates that our season begins, and it is here where we grind away in hopes of glory as State Champions.

—Rivers Townes '09

Commitment to the football program continues to be a source of pride:

During my time in the Upper School, I was part of the football program each year. I lettered on the varsity team in grades ten through twelve. During those years, we enjoyed success that few generations of Cavalier football players ever did. In grades ten, eleven and twelve, our regular season records were 9-1, 8-2, 9-1, respectively. Before then, there had only been three seasons in CCES history with seven or more wins. I believe that our football success was due in large part to the strict off-season programs that began my freshman year. Although we had a coaching change between my junior and senior years, the off-season work continued, and so did our success.

—Ricky Davis '09

The quest for another state football championship lives on.

Students at work in the Cavalier Training Center: "For me, this place is sacred," said Townes.

Team camaraderie flourishes alongside a competitive spirit:

Our coach noted that some teams stretch together. But we devour junk food as our form of bonding before a match. Despite our odd pre-match routine, Christ Church's tennis team is a perennial contender for the State Championship. We like to have fun, but we also have a passion for winning. After warm-ups, we hold hands in a circle and one girl leads a prayer. We then place hands in the center of the circle and cheer "Lady Cavs!" The singles line-up is announced, players from each team shake hands, and the match begins.

—Ashley Robertson '09

The girls tennis team is a perennial contender for the state championship.

The cross country team also finds that friendship binds them together:

The CCES cross country team is very tight-knit. Everyday after school we gather around two picnic tables behind the gym. The atmosphere is akin to a family gathering around the dinner table, or a group of friends who haven't seen each other for some time coming together. There is a reason for the closeness. We have to suffer through grueling practices.

I have learned so much more than the essentials of running from cross country. It has taught me how it feels to eat two hundred peanut butter sandwiches in one month, that it is possible to drink five 32-ounce Nalgene bottles of water in three-and-a-half minutes, that there is no such thing as too much pasta, that pajama pants are both fashionable and functional. Cross-country has been the defining aspect of my Christ Church life. From it, I have gained friends and experienced things that I will never forget and will always cherish.

—William Liston Pitman, Jr. '09

Anticipation of practice is part of the joy of being on the swim team:

Following an eventful day of classes, I scurry home to get a head start on the interminable mound of homework that perpetually awaits me. I delve into United States Government, attempt to solve calculus problems, or read about the "Twelve Labors of Hercules." However, I am greatly distracted by the minutes that pass, readily approaching the time that I can begin to get ready for swim practice. On my way to practice at the Stone Lake Community Pool, I drive on Interstate 385, moving through the after-work traffic. I sing loudly and horribly along with the music that blasts from my car radio, an expression of my excitement that I will be soon with my little "swim team family."

—Marjie Schondelmaier '09

For some students, the joy and camaraderie of athletic practice rivals the excitement of the game.

Students hold aloft the swim team trophies for the 2008 season.

Being part of the state champion soccer team is especially rewarding:

When I am on my way to soccer practice, I get excited. When I am on my way to a soccer game, I get the butterfly feeling in my stomach, not because I am nervous, but because I am excited that I am going to do something that I thoroughly enjoy: playing soccer with friends that play soccer too. After winning eight straight championships, CCES has a record of being competitive with every team in the state.

—Bobby James '09

As enrollment has grown, so has the number of productions staged during the school year. This gives more students the opportunity to participate. This photos is from the 2008 reproduction of Ionesco's *Rhinoceros*.

Drama practices can stretch well into the evening:

Drama at Christ Church is like a chameleon: it is ever-changing, ever-evolving; the plays chosen are always exciting and always, always challenging. So very much goes into a production, and at CCES I have had the opportunity to act, produce, and be on the running crew, experiencing all sides of theater.

The amount of time it takes to put on a production is enormous. Rehearsals and memorizing lines or songs can seem like a never-ending chore. However, the thrill that comes right as the curtain opens is unparalleled. Getting into the "zone" with the entire cast, putting on crazy makeup, and dancing until you feel as if your feet are going to fall off all create an unexplainable high. The lights are blinding and scorching hot, the audience is watching you with anticipation, and all you have to do is remember to breathe . . . and smile!

—Elizabeth Blake '09

CCES has always encouraged students to embrace the larger world beyond the campus. Class trips, service projects, and contests at other schools have long been part of the curriculum. These experiences ultimately create confident individuals who are unafraid of challenges.

Sometimes preparation means "staying up until the wee hours:"

The Christ Church debate team is not about arguing. It is not about padding my resume; it is about having fun. At first, we had debate practices after school a couple of days before a tournament. Preparation meant staying up until the wee hours of the morning the night before the debate. This gradually evolved to practice rounds a week before the tournament and debate 'get-togethers.' Now, it is a given that we hang out every weekend and prepare our cases a couple of weeks in advance.

—Sarah Guzick '09

"A school with more opportunities to pursue a wider variety of activities cannot be found:"

Looking around Christ Church, one sees many different types of talent, from academic to artistic to athletic. Many students find their niche on the field, but many others find their place elsewhere. What I have grown to love about Christ Church is that the School fosters individuality. A school with more opportunities to pursue a wider variety of activities cannot be found. This is certainly good news for someone like me, who feels infinitely more comfortable with a paintbrush in her hand than with running shoes on her feet. I have come to realize that CCES expects nothing more of its students than for them to do their best at what they love. This atmosphere – encouragement do to my best at challenges I can meet – has shaped the person I am and will have a lasting impact on my character and my life.

—Emily Snow '09

LOOKING AHEAD

Fifty years have come and gone, and in that time CCES has solidified a foundation that will sustain it for years to come. But what about the coming years? What will they hold? Dean of Students Wes Clarke (2007–present), is optimistic about the future:

Today's typical student networks socially with others around the world, finds assignments and grades online, writes more words' worth in e-mail and text messages than in term papers, and reads more web pages than pages in bound books. Many of our students and graduates will hold jobs and manage tasks that do not yet exist. For this reason, the development of so-called 21st century skills will be of utmost importance during the school's second 50 years.

CCES is positioned well for the future. Grade-level service projects foster collaboration and a sense of selfless giving. International Baccalaureate (IB) programs at both the primary and diploma level, and through their concomitant influences on campus, emphasize student self-motivation, cultural literacy, and critical thinking skills. Visiting authors and artists-in-residence bring periodic school-wide attention to a specific area of intensive focus, much like case studies. Finally, tenth grade projects and senior theses offer students the occasion for inter-disciplinary exploration and to develop and showcase their individual creativity and entrepreneurship.

Indeed, CCES will prepare its sons and daughters to face the challenges of the future with approaches that remain largely the same: rigorous academic expectations, individual attention from caring teachers, opportunities for growth and leadership both within and outside of the formal curriculum, and a learning environment grounded in the Episcopal faith. These institutional sensibilities will continue to imbue everything we do.

Fifty years ago, CCES was a small parish school whose classrooms doubled as Sunday School rooms. Today it is a thriving center of learning on a seventy-two-acre campus. Its founders could not have foreseen the many twists and turns that have led the School to its place of preeminence in the Southeast. But they would have known that as long as the School remained grounded in the cross and anchor of faith and in the expectation that students would rise to the challenges of a rigorous education, generations of families would continue to arrive at its doors.

FACULTY AND STAFF WITH 5+ YEARS OF SERVICE

Note: Those whose dates end in "Present" were still on staff when this book went to press in 2009.

2004–Present	Lane (Hayden) Abrams	1996–2005	Jean (Forte) Carter	1968–1974	John Gildersleeve
1985–Present	Susanne Abrams	1997–2002	Keyes Carter '89	1981–1992	Charles Glennon*
1986–Present	Juliane Acuff	1978–2001	Betty Cavan	1990–1995	John Grady III
1986–Present	Kathy Adamee	1997–2005	Sloan (Hawkins) Cheves	1996–2001	Butch Granada
1984–Present	Rodney Adamee	1992–1999	Toni Childers	1996–2002	Eliza (Dickson) Gray
2000–2009	Rocco Adrian	1979–1989	William Chilton	1984–1995	Doris Greene
1985–Present	Molly (Hoffman) Aiken	1996–2001	Lee (Jetton) Churchill	2004–Present	The Rev. Richard Grimball
2004–Present	Saba Alavi	1974–2000	Karen Clark	1961–1975	Mildred Grimbell
1999–Present	Sara Allison	1959–1995	Jean Cochran	2003–Present	Janet Gubser
2000–Present	Alice (Trapasso) Baird	1994–1999	Patti Coleman	2004–Present	Eric Guth
1992–2008	Joy (Frazer) Baker	1969–1974	Stephen Coleman	1959–1965	The Rev. Claude E. Guthrie *
1974–2003	Nancy Baker	1997–2004	Grayson Colleran	2002–2007	Rhudene Hall
1976–1988	Montague Ball	1984–1998	David Connor	2001–Present	Dan Harris
1996–Present	Alice (Munn) Ballard	2000–2005	Mary Conwell	1968–1992	Barbara Harrison
1992–2009	Anne Barber	1965–1981	Jim Conyers *	1987–2008	Ashley Haskins
1994–Present	R. J. Beach	1971–1979	Blair Cooper	1976–1981	Mike Hazel
1994–2000	Tanya Beaugez	1971–1979	Charles Cooper	1975–2008	Chris Hearon
1962–1967	P. N. Becton	2000–Present	Kathy Corwin	1991–Present	Val Hendrickson
1967–1973	Jackie Bethea*	2000–Present	Lee Cox	1991–Present	Sally Henley
1959–1974	Rufus Bethea	1981–1988	Benjamin Crabtree	1965–1974	Nancy Hill
1999–Present	Caroline (Hagler) Bethel '87	2002–2007	Marion Crawford '85	1993–1998	Eugene Hindman
1993–1999	Betty Bishop	1962–1969	Margaret Creech	1987–Present	Linda Hindman
1994–Present	Cindy Blackburn	1964–1971	J. B. Crenshaw	1999–2007	Wayne Hindman
1999–2008	Debbie Blackhurst	1987–Present	Chris Cunningham	1993–Present	Joyce Holcombe
1965–1975	The Rev. Charles Blanck	1989–Present	Kay Daniel	1964–1971	S. H. Hollowell
2003–2008	Christie Boulez	1959–1981	Donna Davidson	1991–2008	Nancy Holmes
1992–2000	Anne Bramwell	2003–Present	Deborah Davis	1996–Present	Emmy Holt
1974–1981	The Rev. Canon Allen Bray III *	1975–1981	Mary Dellinger	1996–Present	Greg Hood
2002–Present	Tammy Brearley	1975–1986	Carolyn (Timmons) DeYoung	1991–1998	Athena Hortis
1986–Present	Joe Britt	1959–1970	Jean Dillard	1997–Present	Anne Howson
1978–1998	Becky Brown	1985–1996	Bill Dingledine	1959–1973	Page (Scovil) Hoyle
1983–1996	Terri Brown	1982–2001	Ellen (Jones) Donkle '74	1998–Present	Pam (Matthews) Huffman '79
1987–1997	Chalmers Bruce	1998–2007	Ginny Doolittle	1994–Present	Joy Hughes
1962–1985	Marjorie Buck	1986–1993	Molly Draper	2000–Present	Melissa (Filer) Hughes
1995–2009	Bobby Burch	1985–1998	Rebecca Earle	1987–2004	Rita Hughes
1999–Present	Annette Burdette	1970–1976	Joanne Edwards	2003–Present	Angelika Hummel-Schmidt
1978–Present	Josie Burdine	1995–Present	Jennifer (Parks) Eley '84	2000–2005	Rebecca Huskey
1997–Present	Donna Burns	1996–Present	Kristi Ferguson	1998–2006	Sue Jaggard
2002–Present	Marvin Burns	1970–1975	Mary Folger	1999–Present	Elizabeth (Sterling) Jarrett '82
1996–Present	Betsy Burton	1960–1979	Dorothy Fowler*	1962–1987	Faye Jay
1992–Present	Dee Butler	2001–Present	Andrea (Hines) Fox	1978–1992	Ann Jennings
1993–1999	Miriam Butler	2001–Present	Michael Fox	1991–1997	Bill Johnson
1960–1969	Barbara Campbell	1963–1990	Georgia Frothingham*	1966–1996	Cathy Jones*
1992–1999	Claire Cappio	1960–1979	Shirley Fry	1991–2004	John Jones
2001–Present	Melanie Carmichael	2001–Present	Terri Garvin	1988–1998	Bruce Jordan
1971–Present	Barbara Carter	1990–1998	Anna Gibbins	1998–2003	Jennie Kappel

1996–2001	Michael Kellett '91	
1994–Present	Gayle Key	
1997–2008	Susan Key	
1961–1983	Ruth King	
1991–2003	Toshiko Kishimoto	
1995–Present	Lila (Hewell) Kittredge '78	
1996–Present	Lynn Knowles	
2003–Present	Jeanne Kotrady	
1998–Present	Connie Lanzl	
1991–Present	Jean Lauritzen	
1977–1993	Kristine Little	
1990–2002	Jim Mahaffey	
1997–2002	Gretchen (Bridges) Mahon '80	
1984–1998	Betty Massey	
1998–2004, 2008-09	Dave Mathewson	
1964–1974	Pat McCloskey	
1973–1997	Lynn McColl	
1993–1999	Jeanne McCoy	
1974–1994	Ethel McCreary	
1960–1973	Sarah McCurry*	
1996–Present	Katherine McDonald	
1991–Present	Becky McDow	
1998–Present	Charlie McGee	
1970–1993	Gena McGowan	
2004–Present	Jennie McGrady	
1999–Present	Paula Merwin	
1973–1980	Anne (Smith) Miller	
1999–Present	Donna Miller	
1988–1995	Ernest J. Miller	
1973–1981	Kay Miller	
1999–Present	Tonya Miller	
1988–1996	Lynn Million	
1995–2000	Bryan Mills	
2004–Present	Virginie Mitchell	
2004–Present	Lillian (Prevost) Monroe '93	
1979–1984	Cary Moore	
1962–1968	Mary Moore	
1984–1995	Harold Morgan	
2000–Present	Kimberly Morgan	
2002–Present	Brenda Mullikin	
1995–Present	Marilyn (Wood) Mullinax	
2003–2009	Kay Nichols	
1998–Present	Jennifer Numberger	
1973–1980	Edward Olechovsky*	
1975–1980	Joyce Parks	
1994–2007	Chris (Weatherford) Parsons	

1988–Present	Denise Pearsall
1977–1993	Kristine Petesch
1986–1997	Betty Phillips
2001–Present	Sally (Shurtz) Pielou
1965–1983	Eugenia (Howard Reese) Potter
1969–1999	Robert Powell
1993–1999	Anna (Dunson) Pressly '62
1968–1974	Florence Pressly
2000–Present	Rhonda Pruitt
1999–Present	Donna Qualls
1974–1991	Roxanne Radford
1993–2007	Ronnie Raynes
1968–1974	Allen Thomas Reese
1972–2000	Linda Reeves*
1985–1990	Robin Reynolds
1995–2001	Sabine Rhoden
1995–Present	Ellie Rhodes
1962–1989	Deas Richardson
1997–Present	Valerie (Morris) Riddle
1979–2007	Nancy Riegel
1969–1988	Phyllis Riley
1979–1988	Barbara Roberts
2003–Present	Brent Roberts
1979–1986	Pamela Robinson-Redman
1990–1997	Amy Rogers
1998–2009	Cindy Rogers
1982–1994	Jackie Rogers*
1960–1977	Mary Roper*
1973–1979	Jane Roy
1960–1979	Carolyn Ruff*
2001–Present	Yan Rulli
1988–1997	Jim Rumrill
1976–1983	Caroline (Wood) Ryan
1994–2000	Patrick Schuermann
1985–2006	Helen (Wallace) Schwiers '76
1998–Present	Nancy Scott
1959–1964	Sara Seaborn
2002–Present	Russell Shelley
1959–1970	Genevieve Shirley
1959–1968	Thomas Shirley
1992–Present	Janie Sickinger
2000–Present	David Sims
2000–2007	Bill Sparrgrove
1979–1985	Cary Spears
1976–1989	Harry Sprouse
1974–2004	Diana Stafford

1974–1998	Mike Stafford
1974–1984	Larry Steinmeyer
1994–2000	Bryan Stevens
1963–1970	Michael Stevenson
2002–Present	Leigh Stewart
1993–2007	Margot (DuPuy-Howerton) Stewart
1999–Present	Martha (Gushue) Stone
1981–1986	Sandra Stone
1983–1999	Marshall Stuart
1990–1995	Vicki Sturtevant
1971–2005	Jackie (Fowler, Gaddy) Suber
1981–1991	Ronald Szumilas
1978–1993	Frank Tabone
1994–1999	Bruce Talbot
1969–Present	Ginny Tate
1970–1976	Jim Tate
2004–Present	Viviane (Varin) Till '78
1982–Present	Reggie Titmas
1998–Present	Grace Toler
1984–1995	Teleia Tollison
1999–2006	Tricia Trent
2002–2007	Diane Triplitt
1999–Present	Paul Tutton
2001–Present	Paulette (Bello) Unger
2002–Present	Raeford Vincent
1991–Present	Diane Waldrep
1994–Present	Cary Walker
1981–2006	John Walter '77
1992–1997	Becky Walters
1959–1966	Ruth Watson
1996–Present	Nancy White
1970–Present	Dalton Wilbanks
1999–Present	David Wilcox
1978–1988	David Williams
2000–Present	Jane Williams
2003–2009	Cynthia Willis
2004–Present	Angie Wilson
1999–2005	Jane Wilson
2000–2007	Patrick Wilson
1998–Present	Marsha Winston
1986–1998	James Wood
1984–1995	Kathy Wood
1993–Present	Martha Wrenn
1998–Present	Robin Yerkes
1998–2007	Vanessa (Szatny) Zadel
*Deceased	

SCHOOL BOARD CHAIRS

1959–62	Committee of Vestry
1962–63	Arthur McCall
1963–64, 64–65, 65–66, 66–67	Harrison Trammell
1967–68, 68–69	Randolph Stone
1969–70, 70–71	George Mackey Grimball
1971–72, 72–73	Ben Norwood, Jr.
1973–74, 74–75	Ellison S. McKissick II
1975–76, 76–77, 77–78	Joe B. Pearce
1978–79, 79–80, 80–81	William K. Stephenson
1981–82, 82–83	E. Darrell Jervey
1983–84	J. Maxcy Cochran, Jr.
1984–85	G. P. Apperson, Jr.
1985–86	J. Maxcy Cochran, Jr.
1986–87	W. H. Bard Parks
1987–88	F. Pierce Williams, Jr.
1988–89, 89–90	James B. Pressly, Jr.
1990–91, 91–92	Robert E. Hughes, Jr.
1992–93	Cecil H. Nelson, Jr.
1993–94	Pat Haskell-Robinson
1994–95	William R. Timmons III
1995–96, 96–97	Julius A. Gilreath, Jr.
1997–98	Sallie P. White
1998–00	Robert S. Small, Jr.
2000–01	Julius A. Gilreath, Jr.
2001–04	Frances D. Ellison '68
2004–08	Rodney L. Grandy
2008–09	Edgar M. Norris, Jr.

BOARD OF VISITORS CHARTER MEMBERS

Hugh K. "Bud" Aiken	Joseph L. Jennings, Jr.
George P. "Pat" Apperson	E. Darrell Jervey II
Gordon W. Blackwell	William deB. "Bern" Mebane
Mamie J. Bruce	William A. Mitchell, Jr.
The Rev. Thomas H. Carson	Edgar M. Norris, Sr.
C. Langdon Cheves, Jr.	Patricia Haskell-Robinson
Stewart C. Cureton	Mary P. Sterling
Nathan A. Einstein	E. Randolph Stone
Georgia M. Frothingham	Mack I. Whittle, Jr.
Richard H. Furman	Marguerite R. Wyche '65
M. Dexter Hagy	Samuel L. Zimmerman
Shirley C. Halter	

STUDENT BODY PRESIDENTS 1972–2009

1972	Ed Buck	1991	Robert Lominack
1973	Al Robinson	1992	Bob Croft
1974	Andy Roe	1993	Amy McCauley
1975	Allen Gibson	1994	Brooks Ariail
1976	Lynda Harrison	1995	Matt Cappio
1977	William Stewart	1997	Bentley DeGarmo
1978	Dena Stone	1998	Hal Shaw
1979	David Quattlebaum	1999	Craig Ragsdale
1980	David King	2000	Lucie Burford
1981	Mark Kent	2001	Patrick McInerney
1982	Frank Williams	2002	Kevin Roe
1983	Bibby Harris	2003	Peter Micali
1984	John Jennings	2004	Ward Williams
1985	Chris Roberts	2005	Fletcher McCraw
1986	Will Jetton	2006	Zay Kittredge
1987	Wes Allison	2007	Smyth McKissick
1988	Caralyn Hagy	2008	Chase Carpenter
1989	Katherine Russell	2009	Jennings Johnstone
1990	Kathryn Cheves		

CCES BOYS ATHLETIC CHAMPIONSHIPS 1972–2009

CROSS COUNTRY	SOCCER	TENNIS
1992–93	1995–96	1975–76
2006–07	2000–01	1976–77
2007–08	2001–02	1977–78
	2002–03	1978–79
FOOTBALL	2003–04	1979–80
1977–78	2004–05	1980–81
	2005–06	1982–83
GOLF	2006–07	1985–86
1975–76	2007–08	1986–87
1976–77	2008–09	1987–88
1995–96		1988–89
1996–97		1989–90
1997–98		1998–99
2000–01		1999–2000
2002–03		2000–01
2003–04		2001–02
2006–07		2002–03
2007–08		2003–04
2008–09		2005–06

CCES GIRLS ATHLETIC CHAMPIONSHIPS 1972–2009

BASKETBALL	SOCCER	TRACK
2008–09	2000–01	1977–78
CROSS COUNTRY	**TENNIS**	**VOLLEYBALL**
1996–97	1976–77	1994–95
1998–99	1977–78	1998–99
2004–05	1978–79	
2008–09	1979–80	
	1981–82	
	2002–03	
	2005–06	
	2007–08	
	2008–09	

About the Author and Illustrator

ALLISON BETETTE WARREN '82

Allison Betette Warren graduated from CCES in 1982. She attended the University of North Carolina at Chapel Hill, where she earned a BA in English in 1986. Soon after, she began working for *Campaigns & Elections* magazine in Washington, D.C., and later took a position as Associate Editor of *Trusts & Estates* magazine in Atlanta. Currently she lives in Greenville with her husband and three children.

LYNDI SIMMS '01

Since receiving her BA in Studio Art from Furman University in 2006, Lyndi Simms's pursuit of adventure led her to Nashville, Tennessee, where she now lives, works, and creates. She enjoys gallery representation as well as independent sales and commissions of her artwork, ranging from pastel portraits to acrylic floral and wildlife paintings. Please visit www.LyndiSimms.com for more information.